Taste of Life

Julie Stafford

Greenhouse

the diet

This diet is low in fats, cholesterol, protein (especially animal protein), and highly refined carbohydrates such as sugar. It is high in starches, as part of complex, mostly unrefined carbohydrates, and is basically food in its natural state, eaten raw or cooked, but not overcooked.

foreword

The Pritikin diet is gaining respectability. Some members of that most conservative of circles — the medical profession — will talk to you about it. Both subjective and scientific evidence demands that they should. My introduction to the diet was a list of restrictions — no red meat, no ice cream, no butter or margarine, no this, no that. At first glance there seemed to be nothing left to eat. I thought that I would probably fare better in jail. TASTE OF LIFE will quell such protests. It has a positive approach which will be an encouragement to many. Because a fate *worse* than jail awaits you if you dare to ignore the overwhelming data from many sources which says that the Western World eats too much fat, too much protein, too much salt and sugar — and not enough of the complex carbohydrate found in vegetables, fruits and unprocessed grains.

To be imprisoned by the effects of diet-related degenerative diseases — e.g. narrowed coronary arteries, high blood pressure, strokes, diabetes and even some forms of cancer — can be a fate worse than death (that is, if you survive the increased risk of dying prematurely anyway). The next generation of degenerative diseases is already on the way. In the 21 August, 1982 edition of the Medical Journal of Australia a study of 2596 children in NSW aged 12 to 15 years revealed that the earliest precursors of coronary artery disease were present. 30% were overweight, 8–10% of boys and 2–7% of girls had high blood pressure, 9% had high blood cholesterol levels and 20–30% were smoking cigarettes. The Pritikin Program for diet and exercise has been shown to control weight, reduce blood pressure and serum cholesterol. Degenerative disease does not have to be inevitable.

While an increasing number of enlightened people are starting to follow the Pritikin diet, they are still in the minority. A quick glance at supermarket shelves will soon confirm this. Of the hundreds of cookbooks available there might be two or three that abide by the rules. Starting out, being different, is not made easy for you. Food must not only be nutritious, it must also be enjoyable and its preparation not too difficult. Food must be able to be shared with friends without them thinking 'rabbits' food'. New recipes, substitutions in old recipes, and alternative methods are all necessary if you are to make the change.

Julie Stafford started out on her own. She did not always receive encouragement in her endeavours but her personal conviction and enthusiasm have resulted in TASTE OF LIFE. It will help you make that change to a healthier lifestyle so much more easily. And you will find that there is *plenty* left to eat. Most of the recipes follow Pritikin's guidelines. On the other hand, if you wish to challenge your body's defences on special occasions, there are recipes that will help you cheat — just a little.

TASTE OF LIFE — may it whet your appetite — and make it possible for you to come back for more!

Eric C. Fairbank
M.B., B.S., F.R.A.C.G.P.

First published in 1983 by
Greenhouse Publications Pty Ltd
385 Bridge Road,
Richmond Victoria Australia
Reprinted 1984 (six times)
©Julie Stafford, 1983, 1984

Photography by Paul Tremelling
Illustration by Lowana Cummin
Typeset by Abb-typesetting Pty Ltd, Melbourne
from wordprocessed computer disks
by Dead-Set Publishing Services, Melbourne
Printed and bound by Dai Nippon, Japan

ISBN 0 909104 62 X

Distributed by Gordon and Gotch (Australia) Ltd
Melbourne, Sydney, Brisbane, Perth, Launceston, Adelaide

Distributed by Gordon and Gotch (NZ) Ltd,
Auckland, Wellington, Christchurch

This book is for you; who have learnt that our diet does play an important role in our health . . .

It is not just another cookbook, it is a more positive approach to an overall state of good health.

Most of all, it is for you Bruce, Timothy and Cassie, for you are all an absolute delight to cook for.

contents

Unless the doctors of today become the dietitians of tomorrow, the dietitians of today will become the doctors of tomorrow.

— Alexis Carrel,
Nobel Prize Winner (1935)

We are the cause of our own diseases . . .
We can also be the cause of our own good health . . .

— Leon Chaitow,
*An End to Cancer: A Nutritional
Approach to its Prevention and Cure*

Blessed is the man who enjoys the small things, the common beauties, the little day by day events;
Sunshine on the fields, birds on a bough,
Breakfast, dinner, supper, the daily paper on the porch, a friend passing by.
So many people who go afield for enjoyment, leave it behind them at home.

— David Grayson,
The Friendship Book

Very little is needed to make a happy healthy life.
It is all within yourself, in your way of thinking and eating.

introduction

I would like to share a little of myself with you, for I am not on the list of the world's greatest chefs, nor am I a student of the famous Cordon Bleu cooking schools. I will, however, promise you mouth-watering delights to start you on the road to your improved state of health. My cooking ability, and collection of recipes are newly acquired after much research into diet related to health. It was not until my husband, at the age of thirty years, was diagnosed as having cancer that I began my research into diet related to disease, but most of all, in diet related to an overall state of health. Questions I wanted answered were:

1 Was I bringing about my own early downfall, with the foodstuffs I was eating?
2 If the answer to the above was yes, then where should I start in planning a diet to satisfy which still offered me all the true nutrients for good health?
3 If already in a poor state of health, was it possible to restore the body by changing my diet?
4 Could the power of the mind, in expressing only positive thoughts help the diet work?
5 Is exercise a necessary ingredient to overall good health?

My research has shown me that the answer to all these questions is **yes**. It became painfully obvious to me that scores of people were also looking for answers to the same questions. Unfortunately it wasn't until disease of some sort had affected them that they began to search. This was pointed out to me in the case histories documented in *Nathan Pritikin Diet and Exercise* by Nathan Pritikin, and *Health Facts* and *The Health Revolution* by Ross Horne.

By sheer coincidence, I had the pleasure of viewing Ross Horne on local television. He discussed how his wife's life had been saved after introducing her to the Nathan Pritikin diet after she had had a coronary. This is what led me to research his books further and, of course, discover other people who had had similar successes (with a variety of ailments) after trying the diet.

I have based my recipe planning around the concepts of Nathan Pritikin, a man who has revolutionised the thoughts behind 'diet linked with disease', and 'treatment without drugs', using diet instead. Although I have broken slightly with some of Pritikin's golden rules, I truly believe that if you walk the straight and narrow the greater part of your life, your system should be so well in tune that it can cope with a few small luxury items occasionally.

The Nathan Pritikin diet appeared to me as such a commonsense approach to eating that I couldn't understand why we were not all converts to it many years ago.

The medical profession had a mixed view on the strengths and weaknesses of the diet. Either the medical profession had no time to read another 'fad diet' book, or expressed the belief that I would surely die from the lack of protein, or after reading the book doctors were prepared to admit that they did not have all the answers and, after trying the diet, immediately became converts to the diet themselves.

If you have not already read the books I have mentioned, I would highly recommend them as prerequisite reading before trying the recipes. When you fully understand why we are omitting foods which have been your favourites for years and replacing them with natural foods, then your enthusiasm to try these recipes shouldn't falter.

Health cookbooks in general have ignored the salt, sugar, cholesterol, fats and food additives issues related to health. Most books emphasise the cutting down for a slimming result rather than for overall good health. Vegetarian cookbooks, although emphasising vegetable and fruit content, appear to use an abundance of butter, oils, full cream milk, salt, sugar, eggs and food additives.

This is not a health book as such, nor a vegetarian book. It is, however, a positive approach towards adopting a more sensible down-to-earth way of eating.

You will enjoy learning various cooking techniques such as where the addition of fats is not necessary in the preparation or cooking of foods; how to create a soup which can be a morning or afternoon beverage, a start to a main meal or a meal on its own; how to make salads using various combinations of vegetables and fruits and how to complement them with the addition of a perfect dressing or sauce; how to prepare a wholesome main meal without meat; how to use meat as a flavouring ingredient rather than the main ingredient; how to present pasta and rice as main meal dishes; how to serve a dessert that doesn't require a drowning in whipped cream and sugar to be appealing and cook breads and cakes that don't have an abundance of calories; and how to make interesting drinks that don't have to be alcoholic or sweetened.

Food is a source of energy; it should not only sustain but also satisfy. It should keep us fit as well as alive. It should be filling without fattening. It should provide for easy preparation and an enjoyable experience in the eating.

Not only have I offered you a diet that fills all these requirements, but you will delight in the fact that it will save you money.

Good luck and much health and happiness to you all.

Julie Stafford!

opposite:

tomato soup (p 29); chicken parcel (with tomato and onion) (p 58); garden salad (p 35); winter fruit salad (p 82)

overleaf:

hot curried vegetables (p 69); fresh fruit and yoghurt (p 78)

using the diet

A gradual change to a new diet is recommended . . . this will allow your digestive system to appreciate the changeover without too much wind.

Always keep this recipe book at the front of your collection of recipe books, and when looking for a recipe for whatever the occasion, always refer to it first, before being tempted to go any further.

Think of the food you are eating. Eat slowly. Chew all food well.

When eating out at a friend's home, either eat before going and then nibble on foods allowed, or take your own meal with you. Better still, give your friend a copy of this cookbook.

Always have a pot of soup brewing on the stove, or keep a container of soup in the fridge ready to heat. When feeling hungry or thirsty, remember that soup is an excellent beverage or can be a meal on its own.

Lunches and dinners should always feature a large mixed salad of lettuce and other vegetables, cooked or raw. This will never become boring if you explore all the salad and vegetable combinations I offer you and experiment with some of your own according to your own personal taste. Salads are an important part of this diet. To enhance the salad ingredients with a dressing, they should be lightly washed and dried. A salad shaker/dryer would be an excellent asset.

Eat plenty of wholegrain breads at mealtimes. Serve hot with ricotta cheese and garlic, or slice thickly for sandwiches.

Emphasise the vegetable content of a meal, rather than the meat. Use meat to flavour a dish rather than be the dish itself. Wholemeal spaghetti, pasta and rice dishes permit minimum quantities of meat to be used and are an excellent source of natural high fibre.

Steam vegetables over a low heat to retain their full flavour and nourishment. Balance the green and yellow vegetables with at least one or two carbohydrate vegetables such as potato or rice.

Use fruit juices and herbs to flavour a dish where you would have normally used salt, sugar or other additives. You will enjoy using herbs in your cooking once you develop a taste for them after much experimenting.

Measure out a quantity of meat before cooking it, making sure you allow for the correct amount for each person (approx 125g per person per day). Meats can be cooked then chilled so the congealed fat may be removed and the meat then reheated, or the meat can be cooked separately from the vegetables and spread on towelling paper to absorb fat before using.

In recipes calling for eggs, use the whites only, as the yolks are high in cholesterol and fat. To make up the volume, mix with skimmed milk (about 2 tablespoons) or use double the amount of egg whites.

To sweeten a dish, use grated apple, apple juice, orange juice, pineapple juice (all unsweetened), mashed banana or other fruits.

At all times choose fresh foods when available. If buying tinned foods, make sure there are no preservatives or colourings, no added sugar or salt.

Invest in a food processor to save you precious time in the preparation of vegetables, fruits, nuts, meat, breadcrumbs and herbs.

Make refreshing drinks from vegetables and fruits with the aid of a juice extractor.

Keep a number of air tight containers and crispers on hand as this will allow you to store an abundance of prepared food fresh and ready to eat in the fridge or on the shelves.

stocking the larder

Breads: Buy wholegrain breads or pure wholemeal bread. The coarser and heavier the bread, the better. Choose those breads which are labelled 'without artificial colourings and preservatives, no added sugar or fats'. Most bakeries are now aware of the health conscious and their demands, so if your baker doesn't make a wholemeal or wholegrain bread, ask him to look at the recipes in this book. I'm sure if there is enough demand, he will create a loaf within the guidelines. Although time consuming, bread making can be fun.

Cereals: Buy only ready made cereals that are whole grain without added sugar or salt. All Bran, bran, oatmeal, shredded wheat rolls, Weeties, Vita Brits, muesli, toasted muesli (without sugar) are just some cereals that would be acceptable.

Cheeses: Use only skim milk cheese or low fat cheese, finely grated in recipes where mentioned. Most ricotta and cottage cheeses are low in fats. The fat content in wet cheeses should be less than 1% and in hard cheese less than 10%.

Milk: Buy non-fat skim milk powder and make your own or buy non-fat milk.

Eggs: Only use egg whites in cooking. Use the egg yolks, which are high in cholesterol and fats, in a hair shampoo.

Icecream: There is, as far as I know, only one natural icecream on the Australian market, free of artificial colourings and flavourings. However, it does contain egg yolks and sugar. Try making your own icecream with recipes from this book.

Yoghurt: Buy the low fat, skim milk varieties, plain, savoury or sweetened with fruits, e.g. Yoplait. Yoghurt is extremely easy to make in your own home. Try the recipe in this book.

Flour: Wholemeal stoneground flour, grain flours such as rye, millet and soya flour are used in the recipes. Fine ground flour is used when baking cakes, pikelets and dumplings, and stoneground is used for breads.

Cornflour: Used as a thickening agent.

Herbs: All herbs are used widely as flavouring agents.

Spices: Most spices are used to flavour dishes, but should not be used in excess. Some spices can be an irritant to the kidneys.

Black pepper: Use whole peppercorns in a grinder.

Essence: If using an essence to flavour a dish, be sure it is a true essence and not artificial.

Red meat: Choose the best cuts and remove all visible fats. Even with all visible fat cut off, up to 50 percent of the calories are from fat.

Poultry: Remove all skin and visible fat from poultry prior to cooking.

Seafood: In general, most fish is low in fats, high in protein and the essential amino acids. Fish is especially high in trace minerals. When buying canned tuna or salmon, only choose water packed varieties. Shellfish are higher in cholesterol levels, so do not eat large quantities of these.

Nuts and seeds: These are high in trace minerals and B complexes but high in oil content. Because you are eating the entire nut or seed, you are blending the fibre with the oil, which is an excellent form of obtaining nutrients, but you should still only use small quantities. I have chosen almonds, walnuts and cashews. They should be bought fresh in their raw state and preferably still in their casing. You can dry roast them under a griller.

Legumes: There are a variety of dried beans available, including kidney, pinto, white, black, garbanso, soy beans, lentils and dried peas. They are high in the complex carbohydrates and an important source of fibre. They are excellent in soups, casseroles and savoury loaves.

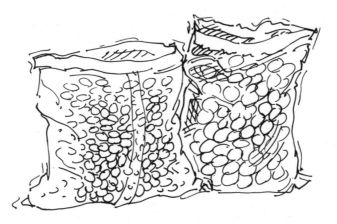

Pasta: Only wholemeal varieties are allowed. These include spaghetti, macaroni, lasagne noodles and noodles made from vegetables.

Rice: Unpolished brown rice.

Biscuits: Some health food stores offer a small variety of bran and wholemeal biscuits. There are also several brands of dry, salt-free crackers on the market such as Rye Krisp, Scandinavian flatbread (Kavli), Ryvita, Finncrisp.

Chips: There are a selection of chips and rice crackers available in health food stores which are a combination of vegetables, unsalted and fat free. The children will love them.

Pastry: You should be able to find a filo pastry which is made from flour and water. However, I find it easier to make your own. Try the pastry recipe in this book.

Vegetables: All vegetables are used except avocado and olives which are high in oil content.

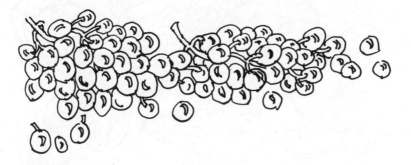

Fruits: All fruits are used and preferably in their whole state. If buying tinned fruit or vegies, make sure they are in their natural juices only.

Dried fruit: Only sun dried fruits should be purchased, otherwise wash and dry all the fruit before using to remove the sugar. These are used in small amounts.

Drinks: Buy fruit juices that are unsweetened and free from colourings and preservatives. Vegetable juices should be free from salt, colourings and preservatives. Dry wine and sherry can be used in moderation. Mineral waters and soda water are permissible. Use tea and coffee substitutes bought at health food shops. 'Nature's Cuppa' and 'Bambu' are two excellent varieties.

Cooking liquids and condiments: Capers, vinegar (rice, wine, cider), Dijon mustard, salt-reduced soy sauce (Kikkoman), lemon and lime juice, dry wine or sherry for cooking.

herbs and spices

- 'Using a little is better than a lot' — herbs are meant to complement a dish, not dominate it.

- Allow quarter of a teaspoon of dried herbs for each four servings.

- Crush herb in the palm of your hand before adding. This gives quicker flavour release.

- Uncooked foods such as salad dressings, fruits and juices need time for the flavours to integrate properly, so add them as long before serving as possible.

- Do not combine too many herbs at one time. Few herbs complement each other. If in doubt, use only one.

- One herb course to a meal is plenty.

- The right herb to use is always the herb that's right for you. Only after experimentation will you become familiar with their strengths and delicacies.

- When using dried herbs instead of fresh, the flavour is more concentrated, so use a lot less.

- Herbs are very easy to grow, inside or out.

- Never oven dry herbs. Hang them in bundles in a cool place or place on brown paper in a dark cupboard to dry.

herbs

Basil: sweet basil has light green, soft leaves. Bush basil has much smaller leaves. When broken and rubbed in the fingers, the foliage has a spicy aroma like cloves. Sweet basil has a slightly stronger perfume than bush basil.
Use: fresh or dry leaves go into Italian dishes, season tomatoes, eggplant, capsicum, vegetable soups, tomato sauce. The fresh leaves are excellent in a tossed salad, potato salad, rice salad, cucumber, cooked green bean salad. Basil is one of the most useful herbs.

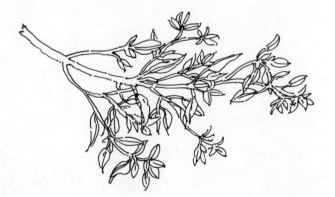

Bay leaves: a bay leaf is added to a bouquet garni, the other herbs being thyme, marjoram and parsley. It is used to flavour marinades, stocks, soups, poultry and fish dishes. Bay leaves may be used fresh or dried, but should be kept in an airtight container.

Balm or lemon balm: this herb has a very strong lemon scent. The leaves are oval in shape and crinkly like spearmint.

Use: fresh leaves are floated on top of cool drinks. Delicious chopped into fruit salad. They give a lemon tang to a tossed green salad. Fresh or dried lemon balm may be put into a teapot with tea as a refreshing pick-me-up.

Borage: this herb has broad, hairy leaves with a cucumber flavour.

Use: when chopped very finely, they make fillings for sandwiches and are good to add to tossed salads. The whole young leaves go into cool drinks.

Caraway: frond-like leaves. The pungent seeds are rich in aromatic oils, and are prized for their use in cooking and as an aid to digestion. Store seed in an air tight container.

Use: breads, especially rye bread. They flavour soups, stewed and baked fruits such as apples and pears. They flavour vegetables such as cabbage, carrots and cauliflower.

Chervil: the green foliage resembles a fine leaved parsley and has a delicate aniseed taste.

Use: the chopped fresh or dried leaves go into the classic 'fines herbes', which comprises equal proportions of chervil, tarragon, parsley and chives. Put in mashed potatoes, green salads, white sauce for fish or poultry.

Chives: onion chives have a round, hollow leaf with a mild flavour of onion. Garlic chives have a flat leaf broader than onion chives and are not such a dark green. The flavour is mildly garlic.

Use: chopped chives go into salads, cream cheese and can be used as a garnish for baked potatoes, soups, entrees, fish, sauces.

Coriander: has lacy, feathery foliage. Ripe coriander seeds are slightly oval, small and a beige colour. It has a spicy aroma.

Use: the ground seeds are used to give a tang to fish, poultry and meat dishes. They flavour cakes, biscuits, pastries and bread. Sprinkle a little ground coriander over apples, pears and peaches while baking. A pinch flavours eggplant and capsicum.

Dill: has delicate leaves of dark green aromatic foliage. Seeds have a pungently dry aromatic flavour (aniseed).

Use: the foliage, either the fresh chopped leaves or the dried crumbled leaves, flavours dips, spreads, sauces, salad dressings, coleslaw, tossed green salads, potato salad, fish and rice. Sprinkle on vegetables lightly. The seeds flavour pickles, chutney, coleslaw, creamed fish, meat loaf, potato salad, cottage cheese, cabbage, cauliflower and cucumber. Dill is an excellent herb used with seafood.

Fennel: the foliage when fresh is chopped finely and sprinkled over fish while cooking, or the whole leaves are used as a stuffing for fish.
Use: the seeds, which have digestive properties, go into pastries and breads, into fish and meat dishes and can be added to steamed cabbage while cooking. They are excellent in beetroot or potato salads.
Garlic: this pungent herb is used in a tremendous number of dishes, particularly casseroles, salads and sauces.
Lovage: the tasty, beneficial leaves of this plant give flavour to soups, vegetables and salads.
Marjoram: oregano and marjoram are closely related herbs.
Use: in pasta and rice dishes, pizza, tomatoes, eggplant, capsicum, zucchini, some meat dishes and savoury sauces.
Mint: a refreshing herb with a cool, clean flavour.
Use: in cool drinks. Excellent with citrus fruit and pineapple, orange and onion salad, new potatoes, peas, carrots, tomato sauces, mint sauce, tomatoes.
Oregano: has a far more pungent flavour than marjoram. It is used with pasta, rice, tomatoes, eggplant, capsicums, zucchini, in pizzas and savoury sauces, and also in some meat dishes.
Parsley: a long time favourite for many reasons. It has attractive leaves useful for garnishes. It has a pleasing taste and contains many health-giving vitamins and minerals. It is also an excellent breath deodoriser after garlic and onions. It combines excellently with chopped chives.
Use: as a garnish or chopped in soups, over salads, vegetables, pasta dishes, rice and mashed potatoes.
Rosemary: the oil in the leaves is very pungent, so use sparingly at first.
Use: chop leaves fresh or dried and add them to stuffings for meat or chicken. Add to potato pastry, spinach, carrots, zucchini, eggplant.

Sage: this is one of the ingredients in mixed herbs, the others being marjoram and thyme.
Use: in stuffing with onions. It seasons breadcrumbs for chicken or fish.
Salad burnet: this herb has soft, serrated fern-like leaves which have a mild flavour of cucumber.
Use: leaves go into tossed salads and iced drinks, and are delicious finely chopped for herb sandwiches.

Winter savoury: the foliage has a peppery flavour. Savory dries easily and will keep its true flavour for a time if stored in air tight containers.
Use: the peppery taste flavours rissoles, savoury mince, beans and pea soups, sauces and salads. The chopped leaves can be sprinkled over cooked marrows, zucchini, squash, beans.

Tarragon: a strong flavoured herb, a little goes a long way. The French tarragon is recommended for culinary use. It does not set seeds. Tarragon must be dried quickly to keep its colour and flavour.
Use: the spicy, somewhat tart taste of the leaves gives a piquant flavour to poultry and fish. Add to a wine vinegar and keep aside for a dressing.

Thyme: garden thyme is the kind most used in cooking. Thyme can be picked throughout the year to use fresh in cooking. Thyme is an ingredient in mixed herbs, together with sage and marjoram.
Use: it seasons meat loaf, rissoles, stews, soups and strongly flavoured vegetables like onions, steamed cabbage, swede, turnips and parsnips. Thyme makes an excellent herb tea.

the spice that's right

Allspice: a spice which has an aroma similar to a combination of cinnamon, cloves and nutmeg. The flavour is strong, so it should be used sparingly.
Use: to flavour chutneys, relish, marinades, cakes and steamed puddings.

Cayenne: a ground spice of the chilli pepper family.
Use: sparingly to flavour seafood, sauces, or as an interesting addition to a basic coleslaw.

Chillies: these can come in whole dried or finely ground.
Use: to add flavour to curries or chutneys or rice dishes.

Cinnamon: this spice is the bark of a tree native to Ceylon. It is presented in a rolled up quill form or finely ground. It would possibly be one of the most popular spices.
Use: adds flavour to rice dishes, curries, cooked fruits such as apples, apricots or pears, cakes and steamed puddings. Cinnamon and orange juice added to a natural yoghurt make a delicious summer refreshing dessert.

Cloves: a spice with a powerful flavour used very sparingly.
Use: whole cloves or ground cloves are excellent additions when cooking apples and pears, to chutneys, steamed puddings, dried fruits and some vegetable dishes.

Coriander: a spice which comes in seed or ground form. It has an orange-like flavour and adds zest to a rice dish or to curries.

Ginger: a spicy warm flavour. For meat and vegetable dishes it is usually teamed with other spices. For desserts, cakes and steamed puddings it should be used sparingly.

Mace: is the outer casing of nutmeg. It has a similar flavour to nutmeg but is slightly more refined. Half a teaspoon of mace is equal to a quarter of a teaspoon of nutmeg.

Use: to flavour soups, vegetable casseroles, sauces, stuffings.

Mustard: comes in seed or powder form. Its flavour is pleasantly poignant.

Use: to add flavour to a white sauce, a mayonnaise or vegetable dishes.

Nutmeg: is most suitably used fresh and grated to capture its true flavour.

Use: a widely used spice in hot or cold drinks, spicy or sweet dishes. Try it with fish, veal, spinach, carrots, cakes and cooked fruits.

Paprika: spice used for its flavour and colour. It is the ground seed of the sweet pepper and ranges from mild to sweet to mildly hot.

Use: flavours chicken, vegetables, fish and sauces. Its bright red colour sprinkled over a pale dish immediately adds warmth and interest.

Peppercorns: I prefer to use the black peppercorn in its whole state and ground.

Use: to add flavour to all meat and vegetable dishes. Black peppercorns are dry, hard and very hot. Green and red peppercorns are soft to touch and not as strong in flavour.

cooking tips

- A steamer of some sort is a desirable aid in the cooking of vegetables. If you do not have one, improvise with saucepans and sit a small rack on the bottom of the saucepan about 6–8cm from the base. Make sure lids fit tightly so you do not lose valuable nutrients in escaping steam. A simple method of steaming is to wrap food securely in foil. This parcel can then be cooked in the oven or barbequed.

- A stiff nailbrush is a useful tool for scrubbing vegetables where it is not necessary to completely remove the skins.

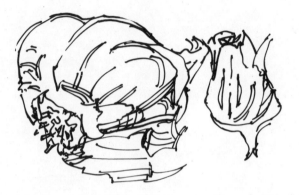

- For easy peeling of garlic, place garlic on a hard board and press down with a knife to bruise the garlic. Skin will peel off easily in your fingers.

- When stir frying in a small amount of water or stock, add the strongest flavours first (e.g. onions, garlic). This will break down the fibres and develop a sauce.

- Cut down the acidity in tomato recipes by removing all the seeds.

- Remove the pith from oranges and use only the coloured flesh. The pith is extremely bitter, especially if you are cooking oranges.

- Wholemeal or rye flours absorb more moisture than white flour, so if adapting old recipes keep this in mind.

- Vinegar in chutney will act as a preservative.

- Gelatin is a tasteless, odourless pure protein setting agent. When adding to another substance, both must be the same temperature ie: add hot gelatin to hot dishes, cold to cold.

- To keep fish in the refrigerator, wrap loosely in plastic wrap.

- Do not wash fish. Leave it to stand in its own juices.

- Smelling fish is the best guide to whether or not it is fresh.

- A fish is cooked when it is white in colour and a fin or gill can be easily broken away.

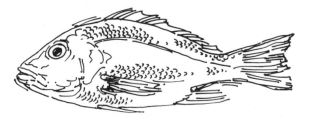

- When baking fish, leave the skin on to hold the shape.

- Remove the skin of fish when stir frying to absorb flavours.

- Fish should be seasoned well, as it can be a bland food.

- Bake fish ten minutes per every 450g. Sauté fish one minute either side. Do not overcook.

- Fish can be marinated up to 24 hours in the refrigerator.

- Chicken can be marinated up to two days in the refrigerator.

- It is a good idea to crumb a fish fillet or chicken breast to protect the delicate meat.

- When crumbing, add flavours to the egg white — dill, lemon juice, coriander.

- Crumbs will stick better if done in advance and rested in the refrigerator for two hours before dry frying.

- Use a metal spoon for folding egg whites into recipes. Wood or plastic will absorb the air.

- Take fresh plums, apricots, etc. to a picnic, or put them in a child's lunchbox, in an egg carton lined with plastic wrap. Then they won't squash.

- To make croutons for soup, place bread squares in an oven and dry bake until golden or, before baking, try spreading lightly with yoghurt, crushed garlic and ricotta cheese.

- To scale fish easily, first dip fish in hot water for a few minutes.

- Why not cook the whole packet of brown rice? It keeps well in the refrigerator in an air tight container and it will be a great time saver.

- Cook a few of the pea pods with the peas to preserve the deep green colour.

- To skin a tomato quickly, hold it over a naked flame until the skin bursts, turning it frequently. The skin will peel off easily and the tomato will not be soggy.

- When cooking rice, add half a lemon to the water. This prevents rice sticking to the bottom of the pan.

- Wash strawberries before removing stems. This avoids loss of juice.

- Homemade breads will keep fresh and moist if wrapped in foil and placed in a plastic bag.

- To avoid diluting the punch too much, use fruit juices for ice blocks or, for an interesting effect, add a piece of fruit such as a strawberry, cherry, a piece of pineapple, to each ice cube before adding fruit juice.

starters

The custom of serving tempting and satisfying foods at before-the-meal gatherings, is a time for cooks to let their imagination and creative sense lead them to express to their guests that they are in for a real treat.

This is a time to take a hold of guests' interest, let them wonder what is to come. Don't share all your secrets and serve just enough to whet the appetite.

broad bean pate

1kg broad beans
125g cottage cheese
2 tbsps chopped parsley

juice of 1 lemon
grated lemon rind
freshly ground black pepper

Cook shelled beans with half cut lemon in water to cover until beans are soft. Drain well and puree to a paste in a food processor. Beat through the cheese, parsley, pepper and lemon juice and rind. Press into a pate dish and refrigerate until well firmed.

Serve chilled with fresh wholemeal bread slices, wholemeal toast fingers or with celery sticks.

brown rice stuffed tomatoes

serves 8

8 medium tomatoes
1 cup brown rice cooked
1 onion finely chopped
⅔ cup currants

2 tbsps pine nuts or almonds chopped
2 tbsps chopped mint
black pepper to taste
½ cup wholemeal breadcrumbs

Slice tops from tomatoes and scoop out pulp with a metal spoon. Combine rice, onion, currants, pine nuts or almonds, mint, tomato pulp in a saucepan and season with black pepper. Bring mixture to a gentle simmer and simmer for 1 minute. Place tomato cases on a foil lined baking tray. Spoon mixture into the tomatoes. Sprinkle breadcrumbs over each tomato. Bake in a moderate oven for 20 minutes or until breadcrumbs are browned.

Serve on a bed or rice.

carrot dip

1 bunch baby carrots
lemon juice or unsweetened orange juice diluted with water

½–1 teaspoon nutmeg
1 cup cottage cheese

Cook cleaned and chopped carrots in equal parts water and lemon juice or unsweetened orange juice diluted with water (enough liquid just to cover carrots). Simmer gently until carrots are tender. Puree the carrots, adding a squeeze of lemon juice, ½–1 teaspoon nutmeg and 1 cup cottage cheese. Spoon into a bowl. Refrigerate until well chilled. Serve with vegetable sticks, celery sticks or salt-free wholewheat crackers.

cheesey pear

per person allow:

½ ripe pear with seeds removed
2 heaped tbsps cottage cheese
Fill pear halves with cottage cheese. Use any combination of the above to garnish.

(Strawberries, grapes, kiwi fruit, orange slices, mandarin segments)

jellied grapes

serves 6–8

enough grapes (preferably seedless) to fill the mould being used
1½ cups dry white wine

1½ cups soda or mineral water
3 teaspoons gelatine

Wash grapes, drain and set aside in refrigerator to chill.

Combine gelatine and ½ cup wine. Stir over low heat until gelatine has dissolved. Remove from heat, leave to cool slightly before adding remaining wine and soda or mineral water. Wet mould being used. Place grapes in mould and gently shake mould to make grapes sit evenly. Pour over gelatine mixture and refrigerate. Serve with a natural yoghurt.

fresh peach or pear appetiser

serves 4

½ fresh peeled peach or pear per person (stone removed)

Filling:
125g cottage cheese
1 tbsp chopped chives

90g chopped walnuts (optional)
30g grated fresh ginger
lettuce leaves for serving

Combine the filling ingredients and mix well. Place a ½ peach or pear onto a lettuce leaf and fill the cavity with filling mixture. Chill well before serving.

pineapple cocktail, frozen

450g can crushed unsweetened pineapple
300ml unsweetened orange juice

300ml unsweetened grapefruit juice
chopped mint to garnish

Mix together all ingredients and freeze until just mushy. Spoon into stemmed glasses and garnish with mint.

This is an excellent refresher to start a meal.

ricotta spread

250g ricotta cheese
1 teaspoon curry powder (optional)

¼ cup date and apple chutney

Blend all ingredients and chill. Pipe this mixture onto salt free dry crackers or into celery sticks.

salmon dip

2 cups drained salmon
225g cottage cheese
3 tbsps tomato paste

1 tbsp lemon juice
black pepper to taste
3 shallots very finely chopped

Blend all ingredients except shallots. Stir through shallots, cover and chill well before serving with a platter of vegetables.

savoury crepes

Crepes:

1 cup stoneground wholemeal flour
1 teaspoon dry mustard

1¼ cups skimmed milk
3 egg whites

Combine all ingredients in a blender and blend until smooth. Let stand for 30 minutes. Cook crepes in a non-stick crepe maker. Pour a little mixture onto the hot surface, rotate the pan quickly to distribute the mixture evenly and pour off excess mixture. As bubbles appear, turn crepe to brown the other side. These very thin crepes take only a short time to cook, so be careful not to burn. Set crepes aside and keep warm.

Fillings:

Mushroom and Walnut Filling:

500g mushrooms peeled and sliced
¼ cup chicken stock
¼ cup finely chopped walnuts (optional)

black pepper to taste
cornflour
fresh parsley chopped

Simmer mushrooms gently in chicken stock. They will make their own juice. Add walnuts. Simmer for 5 minutes. Thicken the juice with a small amount of cornflour and water. Season with black pepper. Fill each pancake with mushroom mixture and sprinkle over fresh parsley.

Asparagus Filling:

1 quantity of white sauce (see recipe in Sauces section)
1 bunch of cooked asparagus

1-2 teaspoons chopped fresh chervil
extra chopped chervil and lemon juice

Combine all ingredients. Fill each pancake with mixture and roll up. Squeeze lemon juice over pancakes and sprinkle with extra chopped chervil.

Chicken and Tomato Filling:

½ cup chopped shallots
1 cup sliced mushrooms
1 can peeled tomatoes and juice
2 tbsps tomato paste

2 cups diced cooked chicken
1 cup cooked spinach
black pepper to taste

Combine shallots and mushrooms in tomato juice in a saucepan. Slowly bring to the boil and simmer for 3 minutes. Add whole tomatoes, tomato paste, chicken and spinach. If mixture is too dry, add water for desired liquid quantity and thicken with a teaspoon of cornflour. Heat through and season with black pepper.

Fish Filling:

1 quantity of white sauce (see recipe in Sauces section)
250g fillet of fish, steamed and flaked
1 tbsp dry sherry or unsweetened orange juice

1 tbsp finely chopped fresh dill
lemon juice and black pepper to taste

Combine all ingredients and heat through. Fill each pancake with mixture and roll up. Squeeze over with lemon juice, season with black pepper and garnish with sprigs of fresh dill.

savoury rock melons

serves 6

3 rock melons halved (serrated)
  with seeds removed
4 tbsps lemon juice
¾ cup natural non-fat yoghurt
1 tbsp lemon rind
1 tbsp basil finely chopped (fresh)
black pepper to taste

1 teaspoon finely grated ginger
2 cups chicken lightly steamed and broken
1 cup green grapes
1 red capsicum seeded and cut into thin strips
1 cup celery threaded and finely sliced
toasted almond slivers

Squeeze lemon juice over rock melons. To yoghurt, add remaining lemon juice, lemon rind, basil, pepper, ginger and chicken. Stir well. Lightly toss through the grapes, capsicum and celery.

Fill the melons with the chicken-yoghurt mixture and sprinkle with toasted almond slivers. Sit rock melons on a bed of lettuce leaves so they do not move about.

sorrel trout terrine

serves 8 as an entree

1½ cups sorrel or spinach leaves blanched for 20 seconds and drained
500g cooked trout flesh mashed or substitute 400g red salmon in water or other suitable fish
1 cup fresh breadcrumbs
2 egg whites
2 granny smith apples peeled, cored and grated
1 tbsp of lemon juice

1-2 tbsps green peppercorns
¼ cup natural non-fat yoghurt
wholemeal French loaf for serving

Place a single layer of sorrel or spinach leaves slightly overlapping in the base of a 10x20cm glass terrine. Combine the remaining ingredients and place half the mixture over the sorrel or spinach leaves, pressing down firmly. Arrange another layer of sorrel or spinach leaves on top of fish mixture. Repeat with another layer of fish and sorrel or spinach leaves. Cover with foil and place in a baking dish containing 2cm of warm water. Bake in the lower half of oven 325 degrees F (160 degrees C) for 40 minutes. Allow to cool and refrigerate overnight. Remove terrine from dish. Cut into slices and arrange on serving platter with French loaf sliced and arranged around.

This would also be a suitable dish to serve as a luncheon idea for four with suitable salads to accompany.

fresh tomato puree

makes approximately 2½ cups

1kg ripe tomatoes skinned and seeded
1 bay leaf
6 peppercorns

6 cloves
¼ cup water
ground black pepper to taste

Place chopped tomatoes, spices and water in a saucepan and bring to the boil over a high heat. Reduce heat and simmer covered until very soft. Puree by pushing through a sieve and discard bay leaf, peppercorns and cloves. Season with black pepper. Cool. Refrigerate until required. Use in soups, sauces and casseroles.

tomato sorbet

serves 6-8

2 cups fresh tomato puree (tomatoes skinned and seeded)
1 cup unsweetened orange or grapefruit juice
1 cup chicken stock
few drops tabasco sauce
1 tbsp dry sherry

1 teaspoon finely grated orange rind
1 teaspoon finely grated ginger
1 egg white
6 small oranges for serving
   or goblets and a garnish of cucumber

Puree all the ingredients until well combined. Pour ingredients into metal freezer tray. Freeze until mushy, stirring occasionally with a fork. Transfer to a bowl. Beat the egg white until stiff and fold into the tomato mixture. Return immediately to freezer tray and freeze until firm.

If using oranges, cut a top off each orange and remove flesh. Chill in freezer until required. Scoop out spoonfuls of tomato sorbet and fill oranges or goblets, garnish and serve.

watermelon sorbet

serves 6

2 litres watermelon puree (approximately 1 small melon)
3 egg whites

finely chopped mint

Place watermelon in icecream trays and freeze. Remove from freezer. Scoop mixture out of trays and fold through egg whites until well combined. Refreeze until required. Remove from freezer to soften slightly before using. Scoop out spoonfuls and serve in bowls with a slice of fresh chilled watermelon and sprinkle lightly with mint.

soups

Soup can be a beverage, a prelude to a main course or a main meal on its own — a versatile dish to warm you in winter or delight you when it is served chilled in summer.

Although the vegetables may lose all their goodness in the over cooking, we can be sure that the stock retains all the vitamins and minerals.

The ingredients of soups don't have to be measured, but it is essential to make a well balanced stock. Too many tomatoes, turnips, onions, etc. may overpower the flavour, and a heavy hand with herbs may offend a delicate palate.

A soup can centre around just one or two vegetables with a particular herb to enhance its flavour; or it can be a combination of vegetables, such as a minestrone served as a meal on its own.

If you have not tried serving soup as a summer delight, then I'm sure the chilled varieties offered in this section will pleasantly surprise you.

Try the addition of yoghurt to give a creamy texture, where you would have normally added cream, or simply puree in a blender for a creamier soup.

Decorate your soup bowl to make it more interesting and appealing: a sprig of parsley or watercress, a twist of lemon peel, a slice of orange, or croutons.

A good cook will surely have a pot of soup on the fire by the day or night, or ready in the refrigerator to be heated at a moment's notice.

almond soup

serves 4–6

1 cup blanched almonds ground
4 cups skim milk
1 leek washed and finely chopped
1 celery heart finely diced

cayenne pepper to taste
¼ cup toasted flaked almonds and ground nutmeg to garnish

Place ground almonds, milk, leek and celery in a saucepan and simmer over low heat until vegetables are soft. Puree in a blender. Season with cayenne pepper. The soup may be served hot or well chilled. Sprinkle with toasted almonds and nutmeg and serve.

bean soup with parsley

serves 6–8

200g haricot beans
1 onion
2 carrots
2 leeks
2 sticks celery

225g tomatoes
2 litres chicken stock
black pepper
6 tbsp chopped parsley

Soak the beans in water for 3 to 4 hours. Using fresh water with a small piece of lemon, cook the beans for 45 minutes or until tender. Drain, reserving the liquid. Peel onion and clean the carrots, leeks and celery. Chop the vegetables except the tomatoes. Grease lightly the base of a saucepan and add ¼ cup stock. Add onion and cook over gentle heat for 2 minutes. Add carrots, leeks and celery and cook for 5 minutes. Skin the tomatoes and seed them. Chop and add them to the other vegetables. Cook for a further 3 to 4 minutes, adding more stock if necessary. Heat remaining stock and make up to 2 litres with liquid from beans. Bring to the boil and simmer for 30 minutes or until vegetables are soft. Add the beans and reheat. Add black pepper to taste, then stir in chopped parsley.

carrot and parsnip soup

serves 4

1 large onion
1 litre water
2 bay leaves
black pepper

½ teaspoon thyme
2 stalks celery and leaves
1 large parsnip
2-3 large carrots

Simmer chopped onion in ¼ cup of water for 5 minutes. Add remaining water, bay leaves, black pepper and thyme. Bring to the boil slowly.

Grate carrot and parsnip and chop celery very finely. Add vegetables to the stock and simmer gently for 1 hour. Puree 2 cups of this soup for a creamier texture. Garnish with carrot curls or finely chopped parsley.

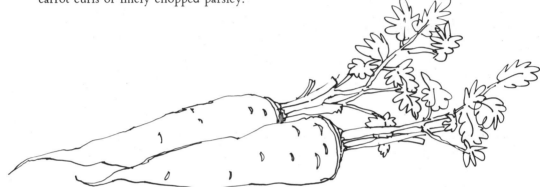

carrot and turnip soup with coriander

serves 4-6

250g baby carrots
250g turnips
1 litre chicken stock
black pepper

2 tbsps non-fat yoghurt
2 teaspoons ground coriander
1 teaspoon ground cummin
1 tbsp finely chopped coriander leaves

Clean and slice the carrots and turnips. Cook the carrots and turnips in ¼ cup of stock for approximately 6 minutes, stirring now and then. Heat the stock and pour it on to the vegetables. Bring to the boil and add pepper to taste and simmer for 30 minutes covered. Puree in a food processor or blender and return to a clean pan. Reheat and add yoghurt and more pepper if necessary. Add the spices and the chopped coriander leaves, mix well and stand for 5 minutes before serving.

chicken stock — basic

makes 1½ litres

2 litres water
any chicken bones, carcass or fresh meat
½ lemon

celery leaves
black pepper

Bring to the boil. Simmer for 1 hour and strain. Store in the refrigerator. Can be frozen.

chicken stock — Chinese

makes 1½ litres

1 kg chicken or chicken pieces
2 litres of water
3cm piece of green ginger peeled and sliced

4 peppercorns
1 onion peeled and sliced
3 sprigs parsley

Bring to the boil and simmer for 1½ hours. Cool and remove any scum.
1   Strain and use liquid only.
2   Remove chicken or meat and puree remaining liquid and ingredients.
3   Leave some chopped chicken in either 1 or 2, depending on the soup you are making.
   This would be an excellent stock for the minestrone soup.

chilled orange consomme

serves 6

5 cups cold chicken stock, well drained
15g gelatine
2½ cups fresh orange juice strained
or unsweetened orange juice

2 egg whites whisked
1 small cinnamon stick
watercress sprigs for decoration

Whisk egg whites into the boiling stock. When stock rises and foams, stir in the gelatine which has been slightly dissolved in 2 tbsps of the boiling stock. Remove from heat and allow to cool for 5 minutes. Strain through damp muslin cloth. Stir in orange juice and cinnamon and allow to rest, undisturbed, until cool. Refrigerate overnight then remove cinnamon stick. Serve in chilled soup bowls garnished with a sprig of watercress and thin slice of orange.

chilled tomato soup with basil

serves 4

1 mild onion
500–700g ripe tomatoes
¼ cup orange juice

2½ cups chicken stock
black pepper
3 tbsps chopped basil

Peel and chop onion finely. Peel tomatoes and remove the seeds. Chop them roughly and combine with onion and orange juice. Bring to the boil and simmer for 6 minutes or until all moisture has been absorbed. Add the stock and pepper and simmer for a further 30 minutes.

   Puree in a blender, adjust seasoning, cool and chill well. Ten minutes before serving, stir in the chopped basil.

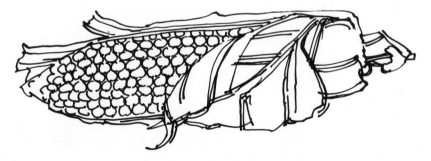

creamy corn

serves 4-6

2 litres chicken stock
3 large potatoes peeled and diced
1 onion peeled and diced
celery leaves

2 cups corn kernels
1-2 cups skim milk
black pepper

Combine stock, potatoes, onion, celery leaves and corn. Bring to the boil and turn down to simmer until potato and corn are tender. Puree and return to a clean saucepan. Add milk, depending on how thick you require the soup to be. Reheat, but do not boil. Season with black pepper to taste.

delicious summer soup

serves 4

500g ripe tomatoes skinned and seeds removed
1 cucumber
1 clove garlic crushed
½ glass dry sherry (optional)

black pepper
4 tbsps non fat yoghurt or
¼ cup finely chopped parsley

Blend tomatoes, cucumber, garlic, sherry and black pepper until very smooth. Chill for several hours. Before serving, stir in either yoghurt or parsley.

Serve with slices of cucumber or finely chopped shallots.

fruity soup

serves 2-4

250g strawberries
2 medium apples

1¼ cups orange juice
¼ teaspoon grated lemon rind

Press strawberries through a fine sieve into a saucepan. Grate the apples and add to strawberries together with the orange juice and lemon rind. Bring to the boil. Simmer for 15 minutes and sieve again. Discard residue and return mixture to saucepan and reheat.

This soup can be thickened with 1 teaspoon of cornflour dissolved in 1 tbsp of orange juice. Stir constantly, simmer 3 minutes more and chill. Serve with slices of orange or a few strawberries.

gazpacho (cold summer soup)

serves 4-6

500g ripe juicy tomatoes skinned, seeded and sliced
1 small onion peeled and finely chopped
1 small green pepper chopped
1 clove garlic crushed
½ cup dry white wine

1-2 teaspoons lemon juice
black pepper
1 can tomato juice (optional)
cucumber slices for garnish

Blend all ingredients except the last four. Add the lemon juice and black pepper to taste. Dilute the soup if necessary with the tomato juice. Chill well in the refrigerator before serving. Garnish with slices of cucumber, parsley or shallot curls.

mushroom soup with chervil

serves 3-4

250g mushrooms
3¾ cups chicken stock
1 cup skim milk

juice of ½ lemon
black pepper
3 tbsps chopped chervil

Wipe mushrooms clean on a damp cloth. Do not peel. Chop them, stalks and all. Heat stock and add mushrooms. Simmer for 15 minutes and cool slightly. Puree in a blender (except for a few mushroom pieces), add the milk and stir until smooth. Add about 1½ tbsps lemon juice to taste and black pepper. Pour into a clean pan and reheat, adding the chopped chervil a few moments before serving. Garnish with spare mushroom pieces.

my minestrone

serves 4-6

2 garlic cloves
1 large onion
9 cups vegetable or chicken stock
2 large carrots
3 sticks celery and leaves
1 large potato
3 small zucchini
10 green beans

½ cup sliced mushrooms
2 x 425g tins tomatoes
3 cups cooked haricot beans
½ cup cooked brown rice or ½ cup wholemeal macaroni
black pepper
1 teaspoon marjoram
any leftover chicken meat could also be added

Crush garlic and chop onions. Cook for 6 minutes in ½ cup stock. Add remaining stock and vegetables, then tomatoes. Season with black pepper. Bring to the boil and simmer for 1 hour, stirring occasionally. Puree 2 cups of soup in a blender and return this to the soup. Add beans, rice or macaroni and marjoram and heat through for further 5 minutes.

parsley and vegetable soup

serves 4

1 onion
2 large carrots
½ parsnip
1 large potato

3¾ cups chicken stock
black pepper
¾ cup parsley (heads only)

Peel and chop onion. Wash carrots and parsnip and chop. Peel potato and chop. Add the vegetables to the stock with black pepper to taste and cook over gentle heat for 30-40 minutes or until the vegetables are tender. Leave to cool slightly. Puree in a blender with the parsley, then reheat adding extra seasoning as required.

parsley chowder

serves 4

1 onion (not too strong)
500-750g fish fillets
500g potatoes
black pepper

2 stalks celery chopped
1¼ cups non-fat yoghurt
6 tbsps parsley

Peel the onion and chop finely. Grease lightly the base of a saucepan and add ¼ cup water. Cook onions over gentle heat until all moisture has been absorbed. Cut the skinned fillets of fish into neat pieces and lay on top of onion. Peel the potatoes and cut them in slices about 1cm thick. Put them in layers over the fish, sprinkling with pepper. Add celery.

Add enough hot water to come level with the potatoes and bring to the boil. Cover the pan and simmer for 40 minutes. When the potatoes are soft, heat the yoghurt and add to the pan. Stir very gently without breaking potatoes. Add pepper and stir in parsley.

potato and dill soup

serves 4

3 cups vegetable stock
½ teaspoon dill
¼ teaspoon black pepper
1 onion

2 stalks celery
3 large potatoes
2 cups skim milk

Bring stock to the boil and add dill and pepper. Chop onion, celery and peeled potatoes and add to the stock. Turn heat down and simmer for 20 minutes or until vegetables are tender. Puree soup. Prior to serving, add skim milk and reheat, but do not boil. Garnish lightly with chopped fresh dill or a single sprig of dill.

pumpkin soup with basil

serves 3–4

500g pumpkin
250g carrots
6 cups chicken stock
1 onion

250g ripe tomatoes
black pepper
3 tbsps non fat yoghurt (optional)
2 tbsps chopped basil

Peel pumpkin and cut into cubes. Clean carrots and cut into slices. Put pumpkin and carrot in saucepan with stock and bring to the boil. Simmer covered for 20 minutes or until soft.

Peel onion and chop finely. Skin and seed tomatoes. Chop them and add to onion. Add 2 tbsps of stock from carrots and pumpkin and bring to the boil. Turn heat down and cook gently for approx 5 minutes until tomato is quite mushy.

Put carrots, pumpkin and stock through the blender. Return this to a clean pan and stir through tomato and onion and juices. Add pepper to taste, yoghurt if desired and basil. Stand covered for 5 minutes before serving.

tomato soup with croutons

serves 4–6

500g ripe tomatoes
½ onion
1 medium potato
2 cups of water
black pepper
squeeze of lemon juice

sprig of basil

Croutons:
wholemeal bread slices
ricotta cheese
cayenne pepper

Peel tomatoes, remove the seeds and chop roughly. Peel onion and chop. Peel potato and chop roughly. Place ingredients in a blender and puree. Place in a saucepan with the water and season with black pepper, a good squeeze of lemon juice and a sprig of basil. Slowly bring to the boil and leave on gentle simmer for 20 minutes. Add more water if necessary.

Spread bread with ricotta cheese and shake over with cayenne pepper. Cut into triangles and bake in a hot oven for 10 minutes. Serve with soup.

vegetable and barley soup

serves 4–6

6 cups water
1 cup barley
2 cups chopped carrot
1 cup chopped onion
2 cloves of garlic crushed
½ cup grated swede

2 cups grated parsnip
1 cup green beans chopped into 3cm pieces
1 can tomatoes
2 tbsps tomato paste
2 tbsps wine vinegar or dry sherry
½ teaspoon dried marjoram

Cook barley in water until soft but not mushy. Blend half the barley with a little of the liquid until smooth. Return this to the soup pot. Add the carrots, onions, garlic, swede, parsnip and beans. Cook until vegetables are tender. Add tomatoes, tomato paste, vinegar or sherry and marjoram. Add additional water if necessary and simmer for a further 40 minutes.

vegetable stock

potatoes
carrots
onions
celery head
celery leaves
spinach
swede
turnip

parsnip
tomatoes
Could also add:
½ lemon
black pepper
¼ cup dry sherry
¼ cup orange juice
¼ cup tomato juice or 4 tbsps tomato puree

All or any of these vegetables in a combination would be suitable to make a vegetable stock. Chop the vegetables and cover them with water and add any extras. Bring to the boil and simmer for 20 minutes. Cover and leave to stand. When cold, strain. Puree the vegetable pulp and set aside. (This could be used to thicken soups.) The strained stock can be kept in the refrigerator and used as a base for soup as required.

vichyssoise

serves 6

4 cups chicken stock
4 medium potatoes peeled and chopped
3 medium onions chopped
3 leeks sliced
1 tbsp orange rind

½ teaspoon marjoram
2 tbsps parsley chopped
150ml non-fat yoghurt
black pepper to taste

Place chicken stock into a saucepan and bring to the boil. Add potatoes, onions, leeks, orange rind and simmer for 20 minutes. Cool a little and place in a blender. Chill well and add marjoram, parsley, yoghurt and black pepper before serving.

salads

Like a soup, a salad can be a meal in itself, a taste tempter for what is to follow, or a small side salad can complement the main meal.

A selection of vegetables and fruits can also be served at the end of a meal to cleanse the palate.

The secret of a successful salad undoubtedly begins with care and devotion to the preparation of either raw or cooked ingredients. Salad greens should be as fresh as possible, washed thoroughly and dried so the flavour and nutrients are not lost.

A salad should be an experience in itself, not simply a nutritious meal. There are untold pleasures in the variety of combinations of salad vegetables and fruits, and all of these should be flavoured with just the right amount of herbs and dressings just prior to serving. If a particular flavour is intended to penetrate the vegetables and fruits, this should be done several hours before the salad is served and chilled.

alfalfa sprout salad

3 sticks celery sliced diagonally
1 cucumber peeled, cut in half, seeded and sliced
6 shallots cut diagonally
10 button mushrooms thinly sliced
1 red skinned apple, cored and cut into strips

2 tomatoes peeled, seeded and chopped
1 cup alfalfa sprouts
salad herbs of your choice (about 2 tbsps)
parsley, chives, etc.

Combine all ingredients and squeeze lemon juice over them. Toss lightly and serve in lettuce cups or on a bed of finely shredded lettuce.

bamboo shoots, carrot and raisins salad

Equal quantities of:
bamboo shoots
grated carrot
radishes thinly sliced

spring onions
raisins
orange rind

Combine all ingredients and use a herb and garlic dressing. Serve this salad in lettuce cups or in a large salad bowl.

banana and celery salad

1 lettuce
4 bananas (not too ripe)
¼ cup lemon juice and ½ cup water combined
3 cups celery diagonally sliced

chopped chives
1 cup natural non-fat yoghurt
black pepper

Set aside 4 crisp lettuce cups. Shred the remaining lettuce finely. Peel bananas and slice diagonally. Soak in lemon juice and water for 5 minutes. Drain and towel dry. Combine bananas, shredded lettuce and celery in a bowl. Mix chives in yoghurt and add black pepper to taste. Add this mixture to the lettuce, bananas and celery and toss well. Spoon equal amounts into each lettuce leaf.

opposite:
salads: orange coleslaw (p 36); orange and mint (p 36); la fiesta (p 35); tarragon vinegar (p 112)
overleaf:
pumpkin almond pie — served cold with salad (p 63)

beetroot mould

6 medium beetroot cooked, peeled, cooled and roughly chopped
2 teaspoons gelatine
2 tbsps boiling water
2 tbsps lemon juice
1 cup natural non-fat yoghurt
½ cup finely chopped parsley

Puree beetroot and set aside. If the mixture is too dry, add a small amount of beetroot juice or dash of white wine to help the puree process. Set aside. Dissolve gelatine in the hot water, add lemon juice. Stir the gelatine mixture through the beetroot. Fold through the yoghurt and parsley. Pour into mould and refrigerate until set. Garnish with slices of orange.

brown rice delight

2 cups cooked cold brown rice
1½ cups corn kernels
1 cup chunky celery pieces
1 cup grated carrot
2 spring onions chopped

Combine all ingredients and toss in a dressing of your choice.

cabbage salad with dill

¼ head hard white cabbage
1 small cucumber
8 spring onions
1 tbsp white wine vinegar
2 tbsps lemon juice
2 tbsps chopped dill
black pepper

Wash and drain the cabbage and cut into thin strips. Peel cucumber and cut in half. Scoop out seeds and cut into slices. Slice the spring onions, using the white bulb and best of the green leaves. Mix all together in a salad bowl. Stir in vinegar and lemon juice and sprinkle over dill and black pepper. Cover with plastic wrap and chill in refrigerator for several hours.

carrot and raisin salad

½ cup raisins
¼ lemon or orange juice
1½ cups carrot, grated or
1 cup grated carrot and 1 cup grated apple

Take washed seeded raisins and soak in lemon juice or orange juice. When raisins are plump, mix with grated carrot or grated carrot and grated apple. Toss through dressing and serve in lettuce cups.

Dressing: combine ½ cup non fat yoghurt, 1 tbsp lemon juice, 1 tbsp vinegar.

cauliflower with herb vinegar

flowers of ½ cauliflower
1 slice lemon
¼ cup mint, chopped
2 cups herbs or tarragon vinegar

Lightly steam cauliflower flowers in boiling water with a slice of lemon. Remove from boiling water and plunge into icy water. Lightly towel dry. Sprinkle with ¼ cup finely chopped mint and toss in herb vinegar. Chill for at least 2–4 hours, tossing cauliflower through vinegar frequently. Drain and serve on a plate or place in a bowl with liquid and put on the table to be served.

celery with herb sauce

1½ cups celery
herb sauce (see recipe in Sauce section)

Chop the celery finely. Discard dark green, tough stalks. Mix the celery lightly through the herb sauce and serve in individual lettuce cups.

chicken caraway coleslaw

½ cabbage finely shredded
6 spring onions diagonally sliced
1 green pepper finely sliced

2 cups cooked chicken
1 tbsp caraway seeds

Combine all ingredients, leaving caraway seeds till last after dressing has been tossed through. Sprinkle caraway seeds over the top of salad and chill well prior to serving.

coleslaw

roughly chopped cabbage
Equal quantities of:
green beans, thinly sliced (cooked or raw)
green peas (cooked)
celery, thinly sliced

corn kernels
grated carrot
red pepper, thinly sliced
chives
cayenne pepper

Combine all ingredients and toss in dressing. The longer this salad chills, the better the flavour. I would suggest at least 2 hours.

Dressing: combine 1 cup non fat yoghurt, ½ small cucumber peeled, seeded and grated, 2 teaspoons finely chopped parsley, 2 teaspoons finely chopped chives, 1 tbsp lemon juice, 1 tbsp vinegar.

cucumber salad, mould

½ cucumber peeled and seeded
1 orange peeled
½ lemon peeled
½ small onion
2 sprigs parsley
2 teaspoons gelatine

2 tbsps hot water
1½ cups mixed grated vegetables
(carrot, cucumber, radishes, green/red pepper)
black pepper
cucumber slices

Juice cucumber, orange, lemon, onion and parsley. Make up to 1¼ cups with water if necessary. Dissolve gelatine into 2 tbsps of hot water. Stir into juice and add 1½ cups mixed grated vegetables. Season with black pepper to taste. Pour into a ring mould and refrigerate to set. Remove from mould and garnish with slices of fresh cucumber wheels.

garden salad

Approximately equal quantities of:
broccoli heads and stems

tomatoes peeled and seeded
onion rings

Place broccoli into saucepan of boiling water and cook for 2 minutes. Remove and immediately place into cold water. Drain water and dry broccoli on absorbent towel. Peel and seed tomatoes and cut into large chunks. Choose an odourless onion or a mild salad onion for this salad. Onion rings can be soaked in cold water and lemon juice to give a crispness.

island surprise

Equal quantities of:
zucchini chunks
carrot chunks
celery chunks
walnut pieces (optional)
orange segments

salad onion in rings
pineapple chunks
1 cup cooked cold soyaroni noodles
capers
parsley

Blanch zucchini and carrot in boiling water for 2 minutes. Run under cold water and drain. Combine all ingredients and toss through a dressing.

la fiesta

Equal quantities of:
tomato chunks
celery chunks
red and green pepper chunks

fresh pineapple chunks
red apple chunks
spring onions or a salad onion

Peel and seed tomatoes and cut into chunks. Add celery. Remove seeds from peppers and cut into chunks. Add peppers, pineapple, apple and onion and toss lightly through a dressing.

mushroom and beanshoot salad

1 cup each of:
sliced mushrooms
red and green peppers

spring onions
½ cup parsley
beanshoots

Wipe mushrooms clean and remove stalks. Cut into thin slices. Wash and dry peppers and cut into thin strips lengthwise. Chop spring onions and finely chop parsley. Combine all ingredients and toss very lightly.

mushroom salad with walnut dressing

250g small button mushrooms
6-8 tbsps white wine vinegar
2 teaspoons Dijon mustard

1 teaspoon date and apple chutney
3 tbsps finely chopped walnuts
black pepper

Wipe the tops of the mushrooms and remove the stalks. Cut the mushrooms into thin slices. Mix together the vinegar, mustard, chutney and then add walnuts. Season with black pepper. Chill the dressing. Coat mushrooms gently with dressing just prior to serving. Serve this salad in lettuce cups.

orange and mint salad

4 oranges
1 cucumber
1 large salad or odourless onion

mint leaves
white wine vinegar

Peel oranges and remove pith. Peel cucumber and run a fork down the cucumber lengthwise, all the way around to give it an attractive finish. Peel onion and slice into rings. Arrange layers of onion, cucumber then orange alternatively in a bowl. Sprinkle each layer of orange with mint before repeating. Pour enough white wine vinegar over to cover. Cover with plastic wrap and chill prior to serving.

orange coleslaw

½ very finely shredded cabbage
2 oranges peeled and segmented
½ cup thinly sliced strips of green pepper

½ cup thinly sliced strips of red pepper
½ teaspoon grated lemon rind
2 teaspoons lemon juice or orange juice

Combine all the ingredients and let stand for 1 hour. Toss lightly in dressing and chill for 2 hours prior to serving.

Dressing: combine ½ cup non fat yoghurt, 2 tbsps orange juice, 2 tbsps lemon juice, 1 tbsp vinegar, black pepper to taste.

parsley and mint tomatoes salad

2 bunches spring onions chopped
125g fennel root chopped
375g tomatoes peeled, seeded and chopped
¾ cup coarsely chopped parsley

⅓ cup coarsely chopped mint
2 tbsps lemon juice
black pepper

Combine all ingredients and add lemon juice. This is a very nutritious salad, full of vitamins.

peach coleslaw

½ very finely shredded cabbage
2 very finely cut apples (strips)

2 very finely sliced salad onions (rings)
4 peaches peeled and sliced

Combine above ingredients and toss lightly in dressing.

Dressing: combine ½ cup non fat yoghurt, 1 tbsp vinegar and 1 tbsp lemon juice

potato salad

washed new potatoes
½ cup finely chopped mint

black pepper to taste
mayonnaise (see recipe in Dressings section)

Cook potatoes in their skins until just tender. Peel potatoes and chop roughly. Add mint and black pepper and let cool. When cool, fold through mayonnaise and chill.

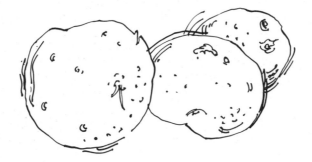

potato salad, hot

washed new potatoes
1 onion
1 green pepper
1 red pepper
celery chopped

grated carrot
black pepper
mayonnaise (see recipe in Dressings section)
parmesan cheese

Cook potatoes in their skins until just tender. Peel potatoes and chop roughly. Finely chop onion, peppers and celery and grate carrot. Combine with potatoes and add black pepper. Pour over mayonnaise and lightly dust with cheese. Spoon into a shallow ovenproof dish and place in a hot oven for 20 minutes or until top is starting to brown.

sesame greens

Equal quantities of:
green beans cut into 5cm lengths
zucchini chunks

celery chunks
lemon juice
2 tbsps sesame seeds toasted

Blanch beans for 4 minutes in boiling water, zucchini for 2 minutes. Run under cold water and drain. Add celery and squeeze over lemon juice. Toss lightly with sesame seeds. Chill and serve in individual lettuce cups.

tabbouleh salad

¼ cup burghul
2 tomatoes peeled, seeded and finely chopped
3 spring onions finely chopped
½ cup parsley very finely chopped

½ cup fresh coriander very finely chopped
cucumber dressing
(see recipe in Dressings section)
crisp lettuce leaves for serving

Soak burghul in luke warm water for 10 minutes. Drain and spread out to dry on absorbent paper. Combine all ingredients in a bowl and mix through gently. Be careful not to make a mush. Add a small amount of cucumber dressing. Serve on a bed of crisp lettuce leaves.

tomato moulds with dill sauce

1¼ cups tomato juice
1 tbsp gelatine
1¼ cups vegetable juice
1 cup cottage cheese

⅔ cup non-fat yoghurt
2 tbsp lemon juice
lettuce leaves for serving
dill sauce (see recipe in Sauces section)

Dissolve gelatine in 2 tbsps of tomato juice. Mix the remaining tomato juice and vegetable juice with the cottage cheese and yoghurt in a blender. Stir in the lemon juice and add the gelatine mixture. Pour through a strainer into moulds. Chill in the refrigerator until set.

To serve, turn onto a bed of lettuce leaves and serve with dill sauce or garnish with sprigs of watercress and a slice of tomato.

vegetable supreme salad

lettuce or cabbage finely chopped
Equal quantities of:
carrot strips
green pepper strips

radish thinly sliced
celery thinly sliced
beetroot thinly sliced
chives chopped finely

Beetroot should be drained, sliced and added to the salad just prior to eating so as not to discolour the rest of the salad vegetables. Combine all ingredients and toss in a dressing. Line a large salad bowl with the outer leaves of a cabbage and fill with the salad.

waldorf salad

Equal quantities of:
apple chunks
celery chunks

lettuce pieces
½ cup walnuts
cucumber dressing (see recipe in Dressings section)

Leave the peel on the apple. A crisp Jonathan or red delicious would be an ideal choice. Cut apple into bite size chunks. Chop celery into bite size chunks also. Tear pieces of lettuce leaves into small pieces. Combine all the ingredients and lightly toss through cucumber dressing.

vegetables

'Does not nature produce enough simple vegetable foods to satisfy? And if not content with such simplicity can you not, by the mixture of them, produce infinite variations?'

— Leonardo Da Vinci

Vegetables offer a variety of shape, colour and texture; they are a presentation delight for any cook, can be served as an hor's d'ouvre, in a soup, an accompaniment to the main meal or, in a combination, become the main meal in itself.

However, of far greater importance is the fact that vegetables contain an abundance of vitamins and minerals. All vegetables should be prepared and cooked properly or they lose their flavour, their colour and their valuable nutrients.

It is not necessary to soak vegetables in water before cooking, as their goodness is readily absorbed by the water. Likewise, do not boil vegetables in water which is then discarded. Vegetables contain a lot of water, so there is no need to drown them in the cooking process. Instead, vegetables should be lightly steamed and still retain a slight crispness.

Unless the skins are hard or inedible, many vegetables do not have to be peeled before cooking, for a great deal of the desirable goodness is in the skins.

You can enhance the flavour of vegetables by adding fruit juices, herbs or a sauce.

Vegetables are an excellent food eaten raw and provide a wholesome between meal snack.

asparagus

Test asparagus for freshness. It is fresh if the heads snap away easily from the stems. The heads are the most tender part for eating. When cooked, asparagus should be tender but still slightly crisp.

To cook, bind the asparagus heads in serving bundles, keeping each bundle the same size. Cooking time will vary depending on the size of the asparagus, but allow approximately 16 minutes steaming time.

When serving asparagus cold, steam it until just tender and quickly plunge it into cold water. Drain and towel dry. Serve with a squeeze of lemon juice, a sprinkle of toasted slivered almonds or a white sauce.

beans

Test beans for freshness. They are fresh if they break cleanly with a crisp snap. Beans have a high moisture content, so are an excellent vegetable for steaming. When cooking beans to add to a salad, lightly steam, then plunge into cold water, drain and towel dry.

beans, ginger garlic

½kg green beans
1 clove garlic crushed
3cm piece of ginger sliced and finely chopped

squeeze of lemon juice
¼ cup water

Toss beans with garlic and ginger and add a squeeze of lemon juice. Add water. Heat wok or large non-stick pan. Put vegetables in and, stirring constantly, cook for 3–4 minutes. Serve immediately.

beans, green, with bean shoots

serves 4

2 cups celery diagonally cut into 3cm pieces
1½ cups green beans cut into 3cm lengths
500g bean shoots

1 teaspoon fresh dill finely chopped
black pepper to taste
⅓ cup chicken stock

Heat a Chinese wok. Add chicken stock. As it bubbles furiously, add all ingredients except bean shoots. Keep ingredients moving while they cook for 2 minutes. Add bean shoots and cook a further 1 minute. Serve immediately.

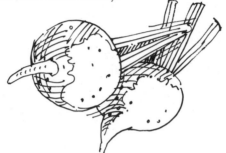

beetroot

The smaller the beetroot, the sweeter the flavour. The skins should be washed thoroughly before cooking. Simmer in enough water to cover until the beetroot is tender when tested with a skewer. To remove the skin, run under cold water and slice.

Try grating a raw beetroot for an added touch to a dull green salad. Or wrap in foil and bake in the oven.

beetroot, baked, stuffed

serves 4

4 medium size beetroots
grated apple
grated onion
chopped celery

chopped capsicum
wholemeal breadcrumbs
squeeze of lemon juice
black pepper to taste

Peel beetroots. Cut the top away and make a hollow through the beetroot using an apple corer. Mix all the ingredients and fill the hollow in the beetroot. Wrap beetroots in foil and bake in a moderate oven in a water bath for 1 hour or until beetroots are tender.

beetroot, sweet cinnamon

serves 4

8 baby beets
1 cup unsweetened orange juice

2 tbsps grated orange rind
1-2 teaspoons cinnamon

Wash beetroot and place in a saucepan. Cover with orange juice and add rind and cinnamon. If there is not enough liquid, add ½ cup water. Gently simmer for 1 hour or until beetroot is tender. Add more water if necessary during the cooking. Peel and serve immediately.

beets, baby, in orange sauce

serves 4

2 tbsps long fine strips of orange rind
¼ cup white wine
1 tbsp cornflour
4 beetroot cooked, peeled and scooped into

small balls using a melon baller
1 cup orange juice
2 tbsps tarragon vinegar

Place orange juice, vinegar and orange rind in a saucepan and bring to the boil. Blend cornflour in white wine and add to the orange liquid. Simmer gently until thickened. Add the beetroot, heat through and serve immediately.

broccoli

Broccoli has a short season, so be prepared for its coming and enjoy its stay!

The florets are most widely used, but the stalks are also highly nutritious. If the flowers are wilting or turning yellow, discard and only use the delicate green tufted heads.

Broccoli only needs light steaming. It has a flavour all of its own, so added herbs or sauces are not necessary.

Broccoli is an excellent vegetable to use in a vegetable combination meal — it will add colour, flavour and interest.

Brussels sprouts

These miniature cabbages grow a thick stem covered with a tuft of leaves and are best eaten when young. Like cabbage, they lose their flavour and nutrients if overcooked. Buy small brussels sprouts and avoid any that are tinged with yellow. This is an indication that they are no longer fresh. Cook as for cabbage, in a minimum of water with the lid on.

Almonds and chestnuts add a delightful change to the just steamed brussels sprout.

cabbage

Cabbage is a versatile vegetable eaten in its raw state or lightly steamed. If it is overcooked, it becomes tasteless and lacks vital nutrients.

The Chinese cabbage is excellent with a combination of vegetables in Chinese style dishes. It needs only light steaming to retain its crisp, nutty flavour.

The red cabbage has a stronger flavour and needs a little extra cooking time, but can also be eaten raw in a winter coleslaw.

Cabbage for coleslaw should be firm with a tight heart. This makes for easier shredding.

Cabbage is best cooked in a small amount of water or stock with the lid on firmly. Let it steam in its own juices.

cabbage, caraway

serves 6

1 small head cabbage shredded
3 tbsps water or chicken stock
3 tbsps unsweetened orange juice
1 tbsp tarragon vinegar

black pepper to taste
1 cup yoghurt
sprinkle of caraway seeds

Place cabbage, water or stock and orange juice in a saucepan. Simmer with the lid on for 8 minutes, shaking the pan occasionally. Add vinegar and black pepper. Cover and cook a further 5 minutes. Remove from heat and stir in yoghurt and caraway seeds.

cabbage casserole

serves 4-6

½kg shredded cabbage (red or white)
2 large onions sliced
2 large apples peeled, cored and sliced
4 large potatoes par boiled and sliced

250 g cottage cheese
black pepper to taste
sprinkle of cinnamon
extra cabbage leaves blanched

Line an ovenproof dish with blanched cabbage leaves. Place a layer of onion and then cabbage, apple and potatoes. Cover with cottage cheese and sprinkle with black pepper. Repeat layers finishing with a layer of potato. Sprinkle with cinnamon. Cover with foil. Cook in a moderate oven for 40 minutes. Remove foil and bake a further 10 minutes until potatoes are lightly browned.

Excellent as a meal on its own with hot bread rolls and an orange salad.

cabbage, sweet and sour

serves 6

½ cup raisins soaked for 30 minutes in
½ cup orange juice
4 cups shredded cabbage
3 onions sliced
4 apples cut in strips
½ cup apple cider

Sauce:
200ml vegetable juice
½ cup unsweetened pineapple juice
215g (½ tin) tomato pieces drained
2 tbsps wine vinegar
black pepper to taste
1 teaspoon cornflour

Drain raisins. Add to cabbage, onions, apples, apple cider. Simmer with lid on for 5 minutes. Add sauce ingredients. Cook a further 5 minutes and thicken with cornflour.

carrots, lemon mint

serves 4-6

½kg carrots cut into sticks
150ml chicken stock

1 tbsp mint chopped
juice of ½ lemon

Steam carrots lightly in chicken stock. Drain. Squeeze over lemon juice and sprinkle with mint. Let stand for 5 minutes before serving.

carrot sunflower seed bake

serves 4

2½ cups carrot sliced
1 small onion finely chopped
½ cup water
black pepper to taste
1 tbsp honey

¼ cup soy grits (ground soya beans)
2 tbsp dill finely chopped
¼ cup sunflower seeds
2 egg whites lightly beaten
¼ cup chopped almonds

Place carrots, onion and water in a saucepan and bring to the boil. Cover and simmer until carrots are just tender. Preheat on very low heat. Stir in all other ingredients except almonds. Pour into a shallow baking dish, sprinkle with almonds and bake for 15 minutes.

cauliflower

Choose a cauliflower that is very white in colour with very tightly packed flowers. This will ensure its freshness. To keep its white colour while cooking, add a slice of lemon to the cooking water.

As with broccoli, cauliflower is also an excellent vegetable to add to a vegetable combination. It will add bulk as well as colour and flavour.

If serving cauliflower simply steamed, it can be given extra interest by adding a squeeze of lemon or orange juice or a sprinkle of your favourite herb.

cauliflower in sesame sauce

serves 6–8

1 cauliflower broken into pieces
1 quantity of white sauce (see recipe in Sauces section)

¼ cup sesame seeds

Lightly steam cauliflower. Heat white sauce. Toast sesame seeds under griller. Place cauliflower pieces in a serving dish, cover with white sauce and sprinkle over sesame seeds. Place in a moderate oven for 10 minutes and serve.

Variation:
Substitute ½ cup raw coconut for sesame seeds. Toast under griller and sprinkle over sauce topped cauliflower.

cauliflowerettes

1 small cauliflower separated into florets
½ cup mint leaves finely chopped
½ cup wine vinegar

½ cup unsweetened orange juice
black pepper to taste

Steam florets and drain. Combine all other ingredients in a bowl and add florets. Toss lightly. Be careful not to break up florets. Refrigerate for at least 2 hours. Drain and serve on a serving dish with a vegetable pie, cold fish terrine, or serve as an entree.

celery

Celery can be eaten raw or cooked. In both cases, it should be washed thoroughly as it is a vegetable that grows up through the soil and pockets soil in its base.

Celery is best cooked by blanching briefly and cooking in a light stock of orange or fresh ginger.

Celery is used in almost every dish, which is probably best because alone it hasn't a great deal of interest.

The aniseed flavour of the fennel plant goes extremely well with celery.

corn

Corn has been a most loved vegetable for centuries. It is very easily grown and should be picked when the silk is still white and the husks are not wilted. The corn should be light in colour and ooze with juice when pierced. Cook by placing in boiling water for 5–10 minutes, depending on the age of the corn.

corn and potato bake

serves 4

2 cups wholemeal breadcrumbs
2 cups ricotta cheese
black pepper to taste

4 cups cooked corn
4 large potatoes peeled and par boiled and sliced
½ cup low fat grated cheese

Spread 1 cup breadcrumbs over the base of an ovenproof dish. Top with a layer of potatoes. Combine ricotta cheese, black pepper and corn and mix well. Spread a small amount over potatoes. Layer with potatoes, corn mixture, potatoes, etc., until all used. Combine grated cheese and remaining breadcrumbs and spread over the top of casserole. Bake in a moderately hot oven for 30–40 minutes or until golden brown.

corn fritters

serves 6

2 cups corn
1 onion finely chopped
3 egg whites
¼ cup skim milk

1 cup plain wholemeal flour
½ teaspoon paprika
1 teaspoon baking powder
black pepper to taste

Combine all ingredients. Drop spoonfuls onto a non-stick pan and cook for 3 minutes and turn to brown the other side.

Serve these with chicken drumsticks and a salad.

onions and leeks

Onions are highly regarded for their digestive qualities and have a high protein and mineral content. They contain their own oil, so there is no need to add oil in their cooking, although a small amount of water can be added if necessary. Cook on a very low heat.

Young onions are the best to use as they are not too strong in flavour. Do not use onions which are soft to touch or which have begun to sprout.

The leek has a subtle onion flavour and is delicious in soups or served simply with a white sauce. Layers of the bulb collect dirt in its growing, so wash a leek thoroughly before using.

leeks, casserole of

serves 4

6 leeks
2 cups celery cut into 3cm chunks
2 cups carrot cut into chunks
2 cups potato peeled and cut into chunks

1½ litres chicken stock
1 tin tomato pieces in juice
black pepper to taste or 4 peppercorns
½ cup chopped parsley

Trim roots from leeks and discard most of the green tops. Split leeks in half lengthways then cut into chunks. Add leeks, celery, carrot and potato to the chicken stock. Simmer for 20 minutes or until vegetables are tender. Place in a casserole, add tomatoes, pepper or peppercorns and parsley. Cover and cook for 30 minutes. If desired, this could be thickened with a small amount of cornflour mixed with some of the cooled liquid.

onions, stuffed

serves 6

6 large onions
wholemeal breadcrumbs
1 grated apple
1 cup finely chopped celery
¼ cup finely chopped almonds

pinch allspice
1 egg white
juice of one small lemon
½ cup low fat finely grated cheese

Peel onions and cut in half crosswise. Carefully remove the centres. Chop the centres very finely and add to breadcrumbs, apple, celery, almonds and allspice. Fill onions with this mixture. Place onions in a pan with 6cm of water to cover base of saucepan. Add the lemon juice. Cover and simmer for 45 minutes. Remove and sprinkle grated cheese over the top of each onion. Grill under a hot grill for a few minutes until golden brown.

Serve on a bed of rice.

parsnip and carrots

Parsnip is an excellent vegetable used to complement another. It is sweet in flavour and teams well with carrots. Carrots contain a lot of natural sweetness and should be selected when young and tender. Wash the skin and do not peel as a lot of the nutrients are found there.

The flavour of carrots can be varied by cooking them in orange juice, squeezing lemon juice on them, or adding lemon rind or orange rind to a stock and cooking them in it.

Chopped parsley, fresh basil and dill or caraway seeds enhance the flavour of lightly steamed carrots. However, carrots are of most value nutritionally when eaten raw.

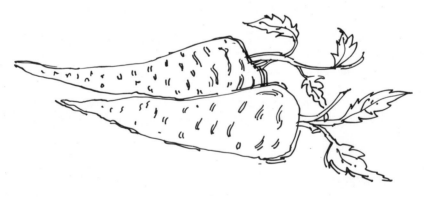

parsnip fritters

serves 4

12 pieces parsnip peeled and sliced into thin rings
black pepper or onion flakes to taste
wholemeal flour

1 egg white and skim milk
wholemeal breadcrumbs

Lightly steam parsnip rings until tender. Drain well and dry on paper towel. Sprinkle lightly with black pepper or onion flakes. Dip in flour, then in egg white and skim milk and coat with breadcrumbs. Gently fry in a non-stick pan until both sides are golden brown.

peas

Peas are rich in nitrogen and mucilage and contain oxalic acid. They can be eaten in the pod when very young and tender, or can be shelled and cooked lightly in a stock. Snow peas are excellent lightly steamed with other vegetables as in Chinese vegetables.

peas, mint

serves 4

Choose very young, tender peas. Shell peas. Allow 1 cup per person. In a shallow pan, pour ½ cup chicken stock. Place enough lettuce leaves on base of pan to hold peas so that they do not actually come in contact with the stock. Add 1 cup chopped shallots and ¼ cup of chopped mint to every 4 cups of peas. Add peas, shallots and mint to the pan. Cover and cook over medium heat, shaking occasionally. They will be cooked in a few minutes.

potatoes

The potato is a prime source of carbohydrate. It should be stored in a cool dry place, unwashed. For full nutritional value, a potato should not be eaten if it is soft to touch or has started to sprout. It is also better to cook potatoes in their jackets. If you need to peel them, do it as close to the skin as you can as most of the nutrients are directly beneath the skin.

When baking a potato in the oven, place a metal skewer through the centre of the potato to ensure an even heat distribution.

potatoes, baked

Peel potatoes and cut in half. Place on a baking tray. Brush tops lightly with natural yoghurt and sprinkle over cayenne pepper. Dry bake in a hot oven until potatoes are tender and tops golden.

potatoes, creamy mashed

Steam potatoes till just tender. Drain and place in food processor. Add skim milk and whizz until desired consistency. Add more skim milk if necessary. Add black pepper to taste and 2 tbsps chopped chives.

For a nutty variation, add 1 tbsp of roughly chopped walnuts.

potatoes, filled, baked

serves 4

Bake 4 potatoes in their jackets in the oven until tender when pierced with a skewer. Slice the top off the potato and scoop out the filling, but leave a firm casing to be filled. Be careful not to pierce the skin.

Ricotta Cheese and Chives filling: combine potato flesh from 4 potatoes, 30g ricotta cheese, 2 teaspoons finely chopped chives, black pepper to taste, 1 egg white.

Tomato Cheese Filling: combine the potato flesh from 4 potatoes, 2 teaspoons tomato puree, ½ teaspoon dry basil, ¼ teaspoon black pepper, 1 tomato chopped, peeled and seeded, and 1 egg white. Fill baked potatoes and sprinkle with finely grated cheese

Apple Filling: combine the potato flesh from 4 potatoes, ¼ cup finely grated cheese, 1 small apple grated, and ¼ teaspoon Dijon mustard.

Celery and Walnut Filling: combine the flesh from 4 potatoes, 30g ricotta cheese, 4 tbsps finely chopped celery, 2 tbsps finely chopped walnuts, and black pepper to taste.

Shrimp Filling: combine the flesh from 4 potatoes, 30g shelled shrimps, 4 spring onions finely chopped, ½ teaspoon lemon rind, ½ teaspoon chopped fresh parsley, ¼ teaspoon cayenne pepper, and 1 egg white.

Return potatoes to the oven and bake in a hot oven for 10–15 minutes or until tops are golden brown.

potatoes, jacket

1 large potato per person

Scrub potato clean, leaving the skin on. Prick potato with a skewer in several places. Place potato in a piece of foil. Grind black pepper over and secure tightly in foil. Cook in a hot oven for 40 minutes or until potato is soft.

Remove from foil. Squeeze an opening in the top of the potato and add 2 tbsps cottage cheese, to which you have added chopped chives.

Other variations:

2 tbsps cottage cheese to which is added: chopped parsley or

1 tbsp date and apple chutney or

1 tbsp grated low fat cheese and cayenne pepper or

1 tbsp chopped celery

potatoes with yoghurt

serves 4

500g small new potatoes boiled and peeled
¼ teaspoon ground cloves
½ teaspoon cinnamon
2 bay leaves crumbled

¼ cup water
½ teaspoon grated root ginger
1 cup non fat yoghurt

Brown potatoes slightly under griller. Add cloves, cinnamon, bay leaves and water to frypan. Stir in ginger and yoghurt. Add potatoes to heat through, but do not boil.

pumpkin

Pumpkin comes in many shapes and sizes. It contains a lot of moisture, so it isn't necessary to add a lot of water in its cooking process. It is best baked dry with the skin on, or cut into small pieces and lightly simmered in a stock or orange juice.

A whole pumpkin can be cored, seeds removed and then filled with a rice or vegetable combination. Let it cook in the oven until the flesh is tender and serve at the table. Or, remove the top, scoop out the seeds and fill with skim milk, yoghurt, nutmeg and black pepper. Replace the lid. Bake in a hot oven until the flesh is tender and present a great talking piece to your guests in the form of 'the soup of the house'.

pumpkin au gratin
serves 4

500g pumpkin
freshly ground black pepper
dash of nutmeg
¼ teaspoon ground cloves

3 egg whites
¼ cup skim milk
¼ cup non fat yoghurt
½ cup finely grated low fat cheese

Peel and slice pumpkin, boil until tender and drain. Combine with pepper, nutmeg, cloves. Place in an ovenproof casserole. Beat egg whites, skim milk, yoghurt and ¼ cup grated cheese. Pour over pumpkin. Sprinkle over remaining cheese. Bake in hot oven for 15–20 minutes.

pumpkin, baked, with sesame seeds

Cut pumpkin into serving pieces. Steam pumpkin in water until just tender, then brush the top of each piece of pumpkin with natural yoghurt and sprinkle with sesame seeds. Cook until pumpkin is tender and sesame seeds golden.

pumpkin fritters
serves 4

8 slices pumpkin (approximately 2cm thick)

Batter:
1 cup wholemeal flour
1 teaspoon curry powder
1 teaspoon paprika

1 cup skim milk
2 egg whites
wholemeal breadcrumbs and sesame seeds

Par boil pumpkin slices to tenderise slightly. Drain on toweling paper. Mix together all the batter ingredients. Dip pumpkin slices into batter and then press into breadcrumbs and sesame seed mixture. Cook in a non-stick pan until the crumb mixture is golden brown. Turn and repeat on the other side.

Served with salad, this is an excellent dish for a quick lunch.

spinach and silver beet

Spinach contains essential vitamins and minerals. An easy vegetable to grow, and most earnest vegetable growers will always have a spinach patch.

It is full of moisture, so needs very little water added in the cooking. Just lightly steam, adding lemon juice or your favourite herb. It shrinks away in the cooking, so you need a large amount for a meal.

Silver beet foliage only should be used and steamed in same way.

spinach buns

serves 6

½kg spinach cooked, finely shredded and drained
6 wholemeal rolls
2 cups cottage cheese

3 egg whites
black pepper
¼ teaspoon nutmeg

Remove tops from buns. Scoop out bread and make into breadcrumbs. Combine spinach, breadcrumbs, cottage cheese, egg whites, black pepper and nutmeg. Spoon mixture evenly into buns and replace tops. Wrap in foil and cook in a moderately hot oven for 30 minutes. Serve with a salad.

tomato, baked

serves 4

2 large ripe tomatoes
1 cup wholemeal breadcrumbs
1 onion finely chopped

½ teaspoon mixed herbs
2 tbsps finely chopped green pepper
¼ cup grated low fat cheese

Cut tomatoes in half. Remove seeds. Combine breadcrumbs, onion, herbs, pepper and cheese. Spoon mixture into tomatoes and bake in moderate oven for 20 minutes or until tomatoes are tender and filling is starting to brown.

turnips and swedes

When choosing turnips, they should be young and tender. Old turnips have a bitter flavour. They can be eaten raw in a mixed salad or are excellent in a vegetable casserole.

Turnips and swedes are sometimes mistaken for each other. Although they are both root vegetables and similar in appearance, the swede is yellow in colour and very much sweeter. Swedes are excellent in soup, especially when grated, in a vegetable casserole, or baked.

turnips in lemon sauce

serves 4–6

500g small turnips peeled and sliced
1 cup orange juice and 1 cup water
2 tbsps orange rind or lemon rind

1 tbsp Dijon mustard
lemon juice to taste
1 tbsp parsley finely chopped

Cook turnips in orange juice, water and rind for 10–15 minutes or until tender. Drain and cover so that they steam themselves dry. Keep ½ cup of liquid that turnips have been cooked in. Blend in the mustard and lemon juice and stir in the turnips. Heat through and sprinkle with parsley just before serving.

turnips, sherry, in yoghurt

serves 4–6

½ kg turnips peeled and cut into strips
1 tbsp dry sherry
black pepper to taste

2 cups non-fat yoghurt
1 tbsp dill finely chopped

Boil turnips in enough water to cover until tender and then strain. Add sherry to the turnips in a saucepan and cover. Let stand 20 minutes. Stir twice to move turnips through the sherry. Add yoghurt and heat through, but do not boil. Add finely chopped dill and serve.

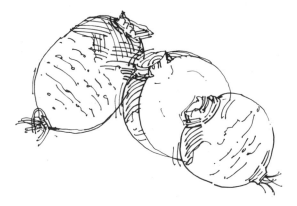

vegetable casserole with orange swede sauce

serves 6–8

4 large potatoes, peeled and cut into large cubes
2 carrots cut into large chunks
1 parsnip peeled and cut into chunks
1 cup celery chunks
1 cup green peas
1 cup green beans
2 tins tomato pieces drained

1 green and 1 red pepper cut into chunks
2 cups unsweetened orange juice
1 tbsp orange rind
2 cups water or vegetable or chicken stock
2 cups grated swede
black pepper to taste

Place all ingredients in a large earthenware casserole with the lid on. Cook in a moderately hot oven for 2 hours. This casserole is ready to eat when vegetables are tender and liquid has reduced into a thick sauce. If a thicker sauce is preferred, add a small amount of cornflour dissolved in some of the cooled liquid.

zucchini and baby squash

Zucchini should never be more than 15cm long. Young and tender zucchini are full of flavour. Any larger than 15cm lose their moisture and can be very woody. They contain a lot of water and need very little added in the cooking.

Zucchini can be cooked whole and served hot or eaten cold with a dressing. They provide an excellent casing in which you can stuff your favourite fillings.

Baby squash, like zucchini contain a lot of moisture. The smaller ones should be chosen and only light steaming is necessary. Sprinkle with your favourite herbs.

zucchini boats

serves 4

8 zucchini
1 onion finely chopped
1 clove garlic crushed
2 tomatoes peeled, seeded and chopped

1 small red capsicum finely diced
1 teaspoon capers chopped
½ teaspoon basil
½ teaspoon orange rind

Blanch zucchini in boiling water for 6 minutes. Drain. Halve carefully and scoop out seeds. Place into a flat ovenproof casserole. Combine onion, garlic, tomatoes, capsicum, capers, basil and orange rind in a saucepan. Stir over low heat until mixture boils. Boil 1 minute. Remove from heat and spoon mixture into zucchini halves. Cook in a moderate oven for 15–20 minutes. Remove and cool slightly. Serve in lettuce leaves.

zucchini omelette

serves 1

3 egg whites lightly beaten with a fork
1 small zucchini grated
2 tbsps parsley

2 tbsps chives
black pepper to taste

Combine all ingredients and pour into a non-stick omelette pan. When mixture is firm, turn over and cook other side. Serve on wholemeal toast or roll up and serve with a salad.

zucchini with fennel

serves 4–6

500g zucchini
lemon juice

2 tbsps fennel finely chopped

Cut zucchini into 3cm lengths and lightly steam until tender. Squeeze over lemon juice and sprinkle with fennel. Let stand for 5 minutes before serving.

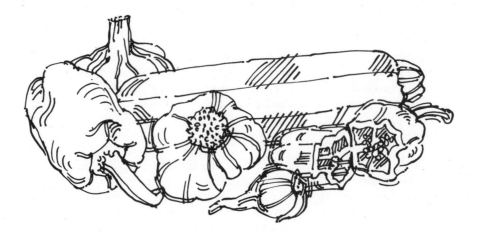

main meals

No longer need you feel inadequate in the kitchen if you do not offer the 'historical' roast for Sunday lunch or when the guests arrive for dinner. Apart from saving considerable strain on your pocket there is much evidence to show that you can improve your state of health by lowering your meat intake to less than approximately 750g per week. This amount allows for an adequate source of Vitamin B12.

Therefore, we must change our old ideas about the place of meat in our diet. Instead of building around meat at each meal time, I tend to use meat as a flavouring agent, emphasising the quantity of vegetables, pasta, rice and breads to make a substantial meal.

If meat still takes pride of place in your home, then it is important to look closely at the methods used to cook the meat. We should at all times be aiming to break down the fat content of meat as much as possible.

Choose lean meats such as fish, chicken, veal and choice beef, rather than bacon, pork, sausages, lamb chops, etc.

By presenting vegetables in a variety of ways, we can create a casserole, a loaf, a spaghetti and lasagne that will leave your guests wondering if there was meat in it or not.

cabbage, whole stuffed

1 large cabbage
Trim base of cabbage. Place in a large saucepan of boiling water and simmer for 8–10 minutes or until cabbage is cooked. To the boiling water, add a bay leaf and a bouquet garni. Remove cabbage from water and plunge immediately into icy water. Remove and drain well. Gently peel back large outside leaves and remove heart of cabbage.

Filling:

500g mince steak or chicken
(or substitute 500g grated vegetables)
1 onion
1 clove garlic crushed
1 small tin tomato paste
1x425g tin tomato pieces drained

1 glass dry white wine
150g uncooked natural brown rice
black pepper to taste
pinch of basil
heart of cabbage chopped finely

Stir fry garlic and onion in 2 tbsps of water or chicken stock. Add minced meat and cook for 2 minutes. Add tomato paste, tomatoes and dry wine. Season with black pepper. When the mixture is boiling, add rice and simmer for 15 minutes. Stir often so the rice doesn't settle on base of saucepan. Remove from heat and add basil and cabbage. Carefully spoon mixture into hollow cabbage. Make sure the cabbage retains its shape. Wrap the cabbage in foil and place in a water bath in a moderately hot oven for 1–1½ hours. Serve with hot rolls and a salad.

caraway and pumpkin pasties

1 quantity pastry (see recipe in Pastry section)	½ cup finely shredded cabbage
1 cup grated pumpkin	black pepper to taste
1 grated apple	caraway seeds
1 small onion finely chopped	1 egg white
½ cup finely chopped celery	extra egg white for glazing

Combine all ingredients and mix well. Cut pastry into squares and mark the squares in half or into circles and mark the circles into half. Spoon mixture on one side and fold over. Press edges together. Wipe tops of pasties with egg white and sprinkle liberally with caraway seeds. Bake in a moderately hot oven for 15 minutes then lower the heat to a moderate oven and cook a further 20–30 minutes.

carrot and onion loaf

serves 4

6 cups cooked mashed carrots	¼ teaspoon cayenne pepper
1 cup wholemeal grain breadcrumbs	4 onions chopped
5 egg whites	black pepper to taste (optional)
½ cup skimmed milk	2 tbsps chopped chives or parsley

Combine carrots and breadcrumbs. Mix well. Add eggs and milk, chives or parsley, onions and cayenne pepper. Mix all ingredients well and press into a loaf tin. Cover with foil and bake in a water bath in a moderately hot oven for 1 hour or until firm.

chicken and carrot loaf

serves 6–8

500–750g minced raw chicken	½ cup fine wholemeal breadcrumbs
1 cup chopped parsley	black pepper to taste
2¼ cups grated carrot (3–4 carrots)	1¼ cups natural non fat yoghurt with
1 small onion chopped	an added squeeze lemon juice

Combine chicken, ½ cup of parsley, 1½ cups carrot, onion, breadcrumbs, pepper and yoghurt in a large bowl and mix well. Press ⅓ of the mixture into a 23x13x8cm glass terrine dish. Sprinkle the remaining carrots over the top and press down firmly. Add another ⅓ of the chicken mixture pressing down well, and sprinkle over remaining parsley. Top with chicken mixture and press firmly down. Cover with foil and bake in a water dish for 1 hour or until golden brown. Leave to cool in glass terrine. Gently ease a metal spatula around the sides of the chicken loaf, turn onto a plate and chill well before serving. Serve with salad and fresh wholemeal rolls. An excellent loaf for a picnic.

chicken breasts in filo pastry

serves 4-6

3 whole chicken breasts or 6 chicken fillets
2 cups grated apple
½ cup roughly chopped walnuts or almonds
½ cup natural yoghurt
2 tbsps date and apple chutney

½ cup sultanas
freshly ground black pepper
200g packet filo pastry
extra yoghurt

Remove skin and bones from the chicken breasts if necessary. Put the chicken between sheets of plastic on a wooden board. Roll out with a wooden rolling pin or beat out with a wooden meat mallet until fairly thin.

Combine apples, walnuts, yoghurt, chutney, sultanas and black pepper. Spread this fruit mixture over the flattened chicken fillets and fold up into a neat parcel.

Brush 2 sheets of filo pastry with the extra yoghurt. Fold in half and brush once more. Place the rolled pieces of chicken on the end of the pastry sheet nearest to you. Fold the sides of the pastry sheet up over the chicken to form a parcel. Continue with remaining chicken and filo.

Place chicken parcels on a baking tray with seam side down and bake in a hot oven until pastry is golden brown and chicken is tender, about 30 minutes. The parcels can be prepared ahead and kept in the refrigerator covered with plastic wrap.

chicken chow mein

serves 8

2 onions roughly chopped
3 tbsps brown rice
1 cup chopped celery
1 cup green beans chopped
1 cup green capsicum chopped
1 cup shredded cabbage

2 cups cauliflower florets
500g lightly steamed chicken pieces
Stock:
2 teaspoons curry powder
2 cups chicken stock
2 teaspoons grated green ginger

Bring stock to the boil. Reduce heat and add all other ingredients except chicken. Cook on gentle simmer for 20 minutes.

Add chicken and heat through. If necessary, this could be thickened with 1 teaspoon of cornflour in ¼ cup of extra chicken stock. Serve on a bed of rice with large chunks of fresh pineapple.

Variation:

Use 500g of mince beef instead of chicken. Add meat to stock and cook gently for 10 minutes before adding the vegetables.

opposite:
vegetables: cauliflowerettes (p 44); baby beets in orange sauce (p 42); baked tomatoes (p 50) filled baked potatoes (p 48); zucchini boats (p 52)
overleaf:
1 picnic: chicken and carrot loaf (p 55)
2 Chinese whole fish (p 58)
3 vegetable fried rice (p 74)

chicken drumsticks

serves 8

16 chicken drumsticks

Marinade:
orange juice
lemon rind
black pepper

Crumbing Mixture:
2 cups wholemeal breadcrumbs
¼ cup bran
¼ cup almonds very finely chopped

Remove skins from chicken drumsticks. Place in a dish and pour over marinade. Leave for 4 hours, turning chicken frequently. Remove chicken. Dip in egg white and roll in crumbing mixture. Place on a foil lined baking tray. Cover with foil and cook in a moderately hot oven for 30 minutes. Remove foil and cook a further 10 minutes or until crumb mixture is golden brown.

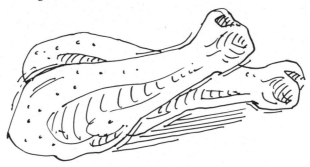

chicken, jellied

serves 6

½ lemon
1x1.5kg chicken
few slices onion
1 small carrot chopped coarsely
6 black peppercorns
few sprigs parsley
1 bay leaf

2¼ cups stock from chicken
6 teaspoons gelatine
½ cup dry white wine
½ small cucumber cut into pieces
1 cup sliced celery
1 medium sized capsicum cut into wedges

Remove skin from chicken. Place chicken in a saucepan with lemon, onion slices, carrot, peppercorns, parsley sprigs and bay leaf.

Add enough water to cover, put lid on pan and cook very gently until chicken is quite tender. Leave in the stock until cool enough to handle. Remove meat from bones and put aside.

Return bones to stock, bring to boiling point, cover and boil gently for about 25 minutes. Strain. Measure amount of stock required, refrigerate to let fat come to surface. Skim off fat. Heat ½ cup of the measured stock, sprinkle in the gelatine and stir until dissolved. Add wine to remaining stock, heat and stir in dissolved gelatine. Pour a little into a mould or bowl rinsed with cold water, chill until set. Chill the remaining gelatine mixture until the consistency of unbeaten egg white.

Arrange chicken and vegetables in the mould or bowl, carefully pour in the gelatine mixture and chill until firm. Unmould on to a platter and serve.

chicken or veal parcels

1 piece of chicken breast or veal steak
(approximately 125g) per person

Marinade:
dry white wine
unsweetened orange juice
lemon and lime juice
dry sherry and apple juice
Herbs:
tarragon
sage

rosemary
garlic
marjoram
coriander
chervil
basil
dill

Marinate the chicken or veal for an hour tossing frequently. Remove meat from marinade. Place onto a sheet of foil and add one or two of the suggested herbs. Add one of the following combination ideas. Secure the parcel tightly and bake in a moderate oven for 30 minutes or until meat is tender.

Variations:
Chicken or Veal and:

fresh halved apricots
stoned red cherries
pineapple and pepper chunks

almonds
fresh peaches
chopped tomatoes and onion rings

Chinese whole fish
serves 4–6

1 whole fish (approx 1.5kg — snapper, nannygai, trevally, teraccihi)
¼ cup lemon juice
4–6 cups chicken stock
1 mild onion diced
1 stalk celery diced
1 carrot in strips
1cm piece root ginger finely chopped
2 cloves garlic crushed
fresh coriander sprigs

Garnish:
1 carrot peeled and cut into matchstick strips
2–3 spring onions finely sliced diagonally
½ cup wine vinegar
¼ cup unsweetened orange juice
Combine and soak for 1 hour.

Clean and scale fish. Rub the fish inside and out with lemon juice. Place the stock in a wok or large deep frying pan. Add vegetables, ginger and garlic. Arrange a rack with chopsticks or place an upturned bowl in the base of the wok. Bring to the boil over low heat and place the fish on the rack. Steam for 20–30 minutes or until cooked. (Alternatively, place the fish in foil in a moderate oven for 30 minutes. Pour over 1 cup of stock and flavourings.)

Place fish on heated serving dish. Bring the remaining stock to a rapid boil until reduced slightly. Spoon over fish.

Drain the carrots, spring onions and sprinkle over fish to garnish. Serve immediately. This dish may also be served cold. After cooking, cool, then refrigerate. Serve well chilled.

fish and asparagus

serves 4

4 fish steaks or cutlets or large fillets
1x310g can green asparagus cut spears
⅓ cup dry white wine
black pepper to taste

4 shallots chopped finely
1 tbsp wholemeal flour
3 tbsps non fat yoghurt
small sprig of rosemary

Arrange the fish in a non-stick shallow oven proof dish. Drain liquid from asparagus and put aside. Scatter the asparagus over the fish, pour the wine over. Sprinkle with pepper and rosemary, cover with foil and bake in a moderately hot oven for about 25 minutes or until fish is tender.

While fish is cooking, stir fry shallots in a small amount of the asparagus liquid or water, add flour and stir for a minute or two. Gradually stir in the remaining asparagus liquid and cook, stirring, until boiling.

Arrange the fish on a heated serving platter, pour liquid from fish into the sauce, stir well, then stir in yoghurt. Gently reheat and pour over the fish.

fish fillets in orange sauce

serves 4

4 fillets of fish (whiting, bream or garfish weighing 125g each, bones removed)
black pepper to taste
½ cup orange juice
½ cup dry sherry
¼ cup natural non-fat yoghurt
1 orange segmented

Season the boneless fish fillets with black pepper. Place the orange juice and sherry in a frying pan. Bring to the boil and add the fish. Reduce the heat to a gentle simmer. Poach fish, turning once until tender. Remove fish and place on a platter and keep warm while finishing the sauce.

Increase the heat and add the yoghurt and boil to thicken slightly. Place the orange segments in the sauce and heat through. Place fish on a serving platter and pour a little orange sauce and some segments over each fillet.

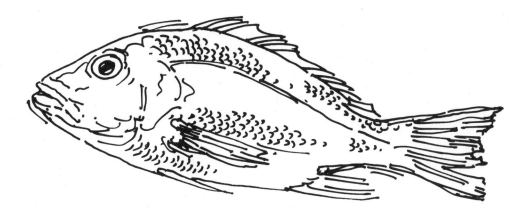

fish in mango sauce

serves 4

8 fillets of whiting (weighing 65g each)
chicken stock

lemon juice
black pepper

Poach fillets in chicken stock. Season each fillet with black pepper to taste and a squeeze of lemon juice as it poaches. Poach for no more than 3 minutes either side. Remove carefully to a heated platter and keep warm.

Sauce:

1 cup dry white wine
½ cup non fat yoghurt

1 mango
black pepper to taste

To make the sauce, use the same pan as the fish has been poached in. Pour out any leftover stock. Pour in the white wine and yoghurt and keep heat on high for liquid to reduce. Add the peeled and sliced mango as the sauce reduces. The mango only takes a couple of minutes to cook, so stir occasionally to move them from the bottom of the saucepan. The sauce takes approximately 4 minutes to cook and will turn a golden brown colour. Place the fish fillets on serving plates and spoon a small amount of sauce over them.

fish steaks poached in lettuce leaves with orange sauce

serves 4

4 white fish steaks or fillets (trevally, barramundi, snapper or salmon)
4 large lettuce leaves (or foil, silver beet, banana leaves)

4 cups water
1 onion diced
1 bay leaf
1 sprig fresh parsley
1 sprig fresh thyme

few slices of lemon and orange
½ cup fresh orange juice
ground black pepper
1 cup orange sauce (see below)
1 orange segmented for garnish

Place the fish on the lettuce leaf and wrap to form a neat parcel. Place the water, onion, herbs, black pepper, lemon and orange slices in a large saucepan. Bring to the boil over a medium heat. Add the fish and additional water to cover fish if necessary. Reduce the heat and keep water on a low simmer and cook fish for 7–8 minutes or until just tender. Lift the fish from the stock with a slotted spoon and place on a serving plate. Pour over the orange juice and refrigerate 3–4 hours. Spoon over the orange sauce and garnish with orange segments. Serve well chilled.

Orange Sauce:

½ cup grated carrot
½ cup unsweetened orange juice
1 tbsp orange vinegar or herb vinegar

1 teaspoon Dijon style mustard
1 teaspoon finely chopped fresh herbs
(chervil, tarragon, parsley)

Combine all ingredients and cook over low heat until carrot is tender and sauce has reduced. Puree and chill.

kokanda (African spicy fish dish)

serves 8

500-750g white fish fillets steamed lightly and chopped roughly
125g freshly grated coconut
1 red capsicum cut into thin strips
1 green capsicum cut into thin strips
2 bananas thinly sliced diagonally
4 medium tomatoes peeled, seeded and chopped
1 cucumber peeled, seeded and chopped
125g chopped fresh pineapple

Dressing:
⅛ teaspoon cummin
black pepper to taste
1 green chilli finely minced
1 clove garlic crushed
1 cup non fat yoghurt
1 tbsp of marinade

Marinade:
4 tbsps lime juice
4 tbsps lemon juice

Shake all dressing ingredients in a jar and let stand 4 hours to let flavours blend.

Mix fish, lime and lemon juice. Leave to marinate for 1 hour in a cool place. Turn fish frequently. Drain. Place in a serving dish and add remaining salad ingredients. Toss well. Pour dressing over salad and chill for an hour before serving. Serve on a bed of crisp lettuce leaves.

pancakes with savoury chicken filling

serves 6-8

1½ cups skimmed milk
½ cup non fat yoghurt
2 egg whites

2 cups wholemeal plain flour
½ cup orange juice

Combine first three ingredients in a food blender. Add flour and blend until smooth. Add orange juice and blend again. Heat a non-stick pan. Pour in enough batter to cover the base of the pan. Pour off any excess. When bubbles appear, turn pancake and cook the other side for just a few seconds to brown lightly. Remove and continue this procedure until all mixture has been used.

Filling:
cold cooked chicken pieces
tomato pepper sauce
(see recipe in Sauces section)

¼ teaspoon allspice
1 cup white sauce (see recipe in Sauces section)
¼ cup low fat grated cheese

Add chicken to tomato pepper sauce, season with allspice. Spread filling in each pancake and then roll pancakes up into tubes. Place pancakes next to each other in a rectangular baking dish. Pour over white sauce and sprinkle with cheese. Bake in a moderately hot oven until well heated and cheese is golden brown.

potato flan

serves 6

1 quantity of pastry (see recipe in Pastry section)

Filling:

2 medium potatoes
4 egg whites
¼ cup skim milk
2 tbsps low fat grated cheese

2 tbsps cold chicken chopped
1 tbsp chopped parsley
1 tbsp chopped chives
1 onion finely chopped
1 clove garlic chopped

Peel and grate raw potatoes. Squeeze dry. Place egg whites in bowl and whisk in milk. Add cheese, chicken, parsley, chives and beat constantly. Add potatoes, onion and garlic. Pour into pastry base in a pie dish and bake in moderate oven for 60 minutes or until well set and browned on top.

potato flapjacks

serves 8

2kg potatoes peeled and grated
1 cup wholemeal flour
¼ cup skim milk
3 egg whites beaten lightly

½ cup chopped onion
½ cup chopped celery
½ cup buckwheat (optional)
black pepper to taste

Add the milk to the flour and mix to a smooth batter. Add the eggs and stir well. Add the celery and onion (and buckwheat if you're using it) to the potatoes and stir in the egg, flour and milk mixture. Combine well. Season with black pepper to taste. Heat a non-stick pan and cover the base of pan with mixture and flatten down. Cook for 2 minutes or until golden brown. Turn over and cook other side for 1 minute. Repeat until all mixture has been used. This quantity should make 16 flapjacks. Keep hot.

Place 2 flapjacks, one on top of the other, on a serving plate, top with shredded lettuce, slices of tomato, cucumber and alfalfa sprouts.

prune luncheon loaf

500g mince steak
3 grated granny smith apples
2 cups mashed potato
1 cup chopped prunes
1 medium onion or
6 spring onions

3 cups wholemeal breadcrumbs
1 teaspoon mixed herbs
black pepper to taste
1 egg white
extra breadcrumbs

Stir fry onions, mince steak and granny smith apples in a small amount of water. Let simmer gently in its own juice for 10 minutes. Combine all the other ingredients and mix well. Spoon into a loaf tin and sprinkle top with breadcrumbs. Bake in a moderate oven for 45 minutes. Serve with vegetables or a salad.

pumpkin almond pie

serves 8

Base:
1 cup wheatgerm
1 cup wholemeal breadcrumbs
Filling:
500g pumpkin peeled and grated
4 potatoes peeled and grated
2 cups wholemeal breadcrumbs
1 onion peeled and grated
1 cup celery finely chopped
¼ teaspoon nutmeg
¼ teaspoon cayenne pepper
4 egg whites
½ cup skim milk
Topping:
½ cup bran
½ cup flaked almonds

Line a round 20cm cake tin with foil. Combine wheatgerm and breadcrumbs. Press down well in the base of the cake tin.

Combine the filling ingredients and mix well. Press this mixture firmly onto the base.

Mix the bran and almonds and sprinkle over the filling. Cover with foil. Bake in a moderate oven for 1½ hours. Remove foil and cook a further 10 minutes until almonds brown slightly. Serve hot or cold.

If you are serving the pie hot, let it stand for a few minutes and pull the foil up and pie can be removed easily and transferred to a serving plate.

roast, corner topside

piece of topside, trimmed of all fat
Cut a pocket in the topside so that it can be filled with a suitable stuffing (see recipes in Stuffing section). Serve with baked potatoes, sesame pumpkin, baked tomato and green vegetables. Place in an oven bag and follow cooking times per kg.

sage and veal loaf

serves 8

500g veal mince
500g chicken mince (or equivalent volume wholemeal breadcrumbs or natural brown rice)
2 egg whites
1 cup rolled oats
1 medium sized onion grated
1 cup stewed apples pureed
black pepper to taste
1 teaspoon dried sage
1 tbsp date and apple chutney
Mix meats lightly with egg whites, rolled oats, onion, apple puree, pepper and sage until well blended.

Pack mixture firmly into a loaf tin (25x12cm). Unmould into a shallow baking dish, brush with the date and apple chutney and bake in a moderate oven for about 1¼ hours.

salmon bake

serves 4

220g tin salmon drained
1 large onion grated
2 large potatoes peeled and grated
2 granny smith apples grated
2 sticks celery finely chopped

3 carrots grated
2 egg whites
black pepper to taste
½ teaspoon nutmeg
lettuce leaves

Combine all the ingredients and mix well. Line a loaf tin with lettuce leaves and spoon in salmon mixture. Press down well. Cover the top with lettuce leaves. Bake in a water bath in a moderate oven for 1 hour or until firm. Serve hot or cold with a salad and boiled new potatoes.

salmon potato casserole

serves 4

220g tin salmon drained
3 large potatoes peeled and thinly sliced
1x425g can tomatoes and juice
1 cup celery chopped
1 cup green capsicum chopped

1 cup grated carrot
1 cup chopped parsley
black pepper to taste
breadcrumbs (optional)

Place a layer of potatoes, then the flaked salmon on base of an ovenproof dish. Cover with layers of tomatoes, celery, capsicum and carrot. Sprinkle with parsley and season with black pepper. Repeat layers until all vegetables are used. Sprinkle breadcrumbs over the top and cook in a moderate oven for approximately 40 minutes or until breadcrumbs are golden brown. Serve with lightly steamed broccoli and hot wholemeal rolls.

savoury mince

serves 4

250g mince meat
1 clove garlic crushed
1 large onion finely chopped
1 cup finely chopped celery
1 cup grated carrot
½ cup sultanas or raisins

1 cup bran
black pepper to taste
½ cup tomato paste
1x425g can whole tomatoes and juice
1 cup chicken stock or water

Stir fry garlic, onion and meat in 2 tbsps water. Add all the other ingredients and gently simmer, covered, for 30 minutes. Serve on wholemeal toast or with rice.

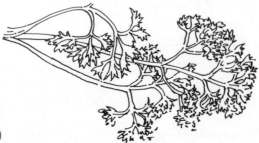

opposite:
vegetable lasagne (p 69)
overleaf:
spaghetti (p 66)

steamed whole chicken

serves 4-6

1 chicken
½ lemon
¼ cup unsweetened orange juice
or ¼ cup apple juice or ¼ cup dry wine
1½ cups water

sprigs of parsley
stick of celery with leaves
½ carrot
black pepper

Completely remove all skin from chicken and any visible fat pockets.

Place chicken in a saucepan that it fits neatly into without legs and wings coming adrift in the cooking. Place lemon in chicken cavity and pour over liquid. Place parsley, celery and carrot in saucepan around chicken and season with black pepper. Bring to the boil. Turn heat down to its lowest and simmer for 30 minutes with the lid on. Test to see if chicken is cooked and remove from stock. Wrap up securely in foil and leave to cool.

Variation:

Garlic Chicken

Wipe the inside of the chicken with 2 cloves of crushed garlic. Follow instructions for above but leave out the last four ingredients.

soy bean patties

serves 4-6

500g dried soy beans
2 medium onions chopped
1 tbsp chopped parsley
1 cup mashed potato
1 cup egg white

1 tbsp tomato sauce (see recipe in Sauce section)
black pepper to taste
wholemeal flour
egg white and 2 tbsps skim milk beaten
wholemeal breadcrumbs

Place beans in saucepan and cover with water to come 2-3cm above level of beans. Bring to the boil and boil for 1 minute. Remove from heat, cover and allow to stand for 1 hour. This is the equivalent for overnight soaking. Continue cooking in the same water for 2½ hours or until beans are tender.

Drain and mash beans well. Combine with onions, parsley, potato, egg white, tomato sauce and pepper. Form into patties, coat with flour, dip into egg white and skim milk and coat with breadcrumbs. Fry in a non-stick pan until golden brown on both sides and serve with a tossed green salad.

spaghetti and meatballs

serves 8
1 quantity wholemeal spaghetti to serve 8

Meat Balls:

250g fat free ground beef
1 onion finely minced
1 mashed banana
1 apple finely grated
black pepper to taste

Combine all ingredients and roll into very small balls. Place in a frypan in 3cm of water which has been boiled and is just simmering. Cook for 8 minutes, turning once. Remove from pan and drain well. Keep hot.

Tomato Sauce:

1 onion diced
½ green pepper finely diced
1 stalk celery finely diced
425g tin tomatoes chopped
2 tbsps tomato paste
1 clove garlic crushed
½ teaspoon basil
½ teaspoon oregano
black pepper to taste
chopped fresh parsley to garnish

Stir fry onion, green pepper and celery in 2 tbsps water for 3 minutes. Add all other ingredients and cook for 40 minutes on simmer.

Place hot spaghetti on serving plates, divide the meatballs evenly and pour over the tomato sauce.

spaghetti and spinach sauce

serves 6
1 quantity of wholemeal spaghetti

Sauce:

2 bunches spinach (16 stalks approximately) washed
or silver beet
2 cloves garlic
60g pine nuts
2 teaspoons chopped fresh basil
or ½ teaspoon dry basil
¼ cup chopped parsley
black pepper to taste

Wash spinach and remove white stalks if using silver beet. Place spinach leaves in water in a saucepan. Cover and bring to the boil. Reduce heat and simmer for 5 minutes. Put spinach in blender with crushed garlic, pine nuts, basil and parsley. Blend until smooth using a little of the cooking liquid if necessary. Season with black pepper.

Place spaghetti on serving plates and spoon over spinach sauce.

spaghetti with tomato and mushroom sauce

serves 8

1 quantity wholemeal spaghetti to serve 8
Sauce:
1 large onion chopped
1 green pepper chopped
2 stalks celery chopped
1 cup finely sliced mushrooms
1 cup grated carrot
425g tin tomatoes and juice

¼ cup tomato paste
1 cup water/dry wine
2 cloves garlic
½–1 teaspoon basil
½–1 teaspoon oregano
2 bay leaves
black pepper to taste

Stir fry onion, green pepper, celery, mushrooms and carrot in ¼ cup water for 5 minutes. Add all other ingredients and cook gently with the lid on for 1 hour.

Topping:
1 cup fine wholemeal breadcrumbs
½ cup low fat grated cheese (optional)

Combine spaghetti and sauce in an ovenproof dish. Sprinkle over topping and cook in a moderately hot oven until topping has lightly browned (approximately 20 mins), or serve spaghetti in a serving dish, with sauce on top.

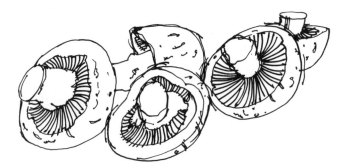

tuna cakes

makes 12

250g tuna in water, drained
4 large potatoes
2 spring onions, finely chopped
2 carrots, grated
½ lemon

1 cup ricotta cheese
1 egg white unbeaten
black pepper to taste
wholemeal breadcrumbs
1 extra egg white and water

Peel potatoes and boil until tender. Drain most of excess moisture away and mash. Leave to cool. Add tuna to potato and squeeze lemon juice over. Add spring onions, carrots, ricotta cheese, unbeaten egg white and black pepper. Mix thoroughly. Take spoonfuls and roll in hands, then dip in egg white and water and roll in breadcrumbs. Shape into round cakes approximately 7cm in diameter. Set the cakes to chill and firm in the refrigerator for 2 hours prior to cooking. This should prevent the cakes from losing the breadcrumb mixture in the cooking. Dry bake in a frypan on moderate heat for 4 minutes either side or until golden brown.

vegetables, buffet

serves 6

4 large potatoes
2-3 small carrots
3 zucchini
2 cups peas
2 peppers — one red, one green
2 stalks celery

2 tomatoes
2 tbsps parsley finely chopped
2 tbsps chives finely chopped
5 teaspoons gelatine
½ cup chicken stock
½ cup dry white wine

Peel potatoes and cut into large cubes. Wash carrots and cut into small rounds. Cut zucchini into rounds. Place these vegetables in a pot of boiling water with peas and boil for 3 minutes. Remove and plunge into cold water and drain. Chop peppers and celery. Peel tomatoes and remove seeds. Chop tomatoes into cube shapes. Sprinkle over parsley and chives. Let stand.

Combine gelatine with ½ cup chicken stock. Dissolve over a low heat. Add remaining stock and white wine. Leave to cool slightly. Wet the inside of a mould or glass terrine dish. Pour a small amount of the gelatine mixture in to cover the base of the mould or dish. Place this in the refrigerator to set slightly.

Arrange vegetables in mould or dish according to your eye and pour over the remaining gelatine mixture. Place in refrigerator for at least 2 hours or until required. Serve with a hot potato salad and green salad and hot wholemeal rolls.

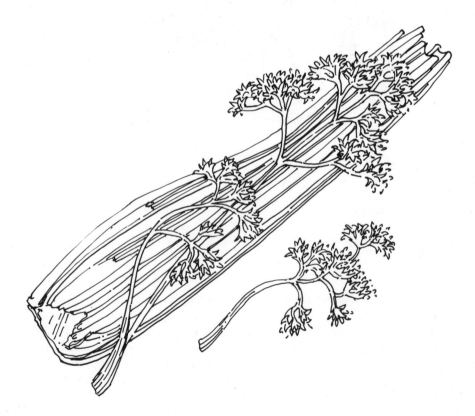

vegetables, hot, curried

serves 4

2 cups chicken stock
1 clove garlic crushed
1 teaspoon turmeric
¾ teaspoon chilli powder

½ teaspoon ground ginger
or 1 teaspoon grated fresh ginger
1 teaspoon ground coriander

(If you do not like very hot curries, use only half the measurements given. If you are using fresh ginger you can still use a full teaspoon measure.)

Vegetables:

Equal quantity of:
carrot strips
zucchini cut into 3cm lengths
celery cut diagonally
green beans cut into 3cm lengths

cauliflower rosettes
red and green pepper strips
mushrooms peeled and sliced
1 375g tin whole tomatoes and juice
½ cup chopped shallots

Bring stock and spices to the boil. Turn down heat. Add vegetables and simmer until vegetables are just tender. Add tin of tomatoes and shallots and heat through. Serve with rice or noodles, and a tossed green salad, a bowl of chilled apple slices and a bowl of cucumber yoghurt.

vegetable lasagne

You can buy a vegetable lasagne noodle. However, an interesting change can be achieved by using peta bread as the noodles. Cut them into rectangular shapes to fit the casserole you are using.

Vegetable Sauce:

1 onion finely chopped
2 cloves garlic crushed
2 granny smith apples grated
2 medium carrots grated
1 cup finely chopped celery
½ cup finely chopped red pepper
2x425g cans tomatoes chopped
3 tbsps tomato paste
1 teaspoon oregano

½ teaspoon basil
½ teaspoon rosemary
black pepper to taste

Cheese Sauce:
Combine the following:
1 cup white sauce (see recipe in Sauces section)
125g finely grated low fat cheese
2 cups ricotta cheese
extra finely grated cheese

In an oblong baking dish, place alternate layers of peta bread, vegetable sauce, cheese sauce and repeat until all sauces have been used. Finish with a layer of peta bread and sprinkle over extra finely grated cheese. Cook in a moderately hot oven for 20 minutes or until cheese has melted and is golden brown.

zucchini au gratin

serves 8

2 cups uncooked brown rice
500–750g zucchini
3 onions
2x425g can tomatoes drained and chopped
4 egg whites
2 cups skim milk
½ teaspoon dried thyme

¼ teaspoon dried basil
½ teaspoon dried oregano
½ teaspoon grated nutmeg
black pepper to taste
1 cup low fat grated cheese
2 cups wholemeal breadcrumbs

Spread rice in bottom of an ovenproof serving dish. Cut zucchini into 1cm slices, slice onions finely. Spread half the tomatoes over the rice and add zucchini and onions in layers. Add remaining tomatoes.

Beat egg whites with milk and add the seasonings and half the cheese and stir to combine. Pour the mixture over the vegetables, using a fork to ensure the liquid penetrates the whole dish. Cover with remaining combined cheese and breadcrumbs. Bake in a moderate oven for 45–50 minutes or until top is lightly browned. Serve with a salad.

pasta and rice

Pasta is now available in many varieties in a wholewheat flour form. These include spaghetti, buckwheat noodles (soba), soyaroni, vegeroni, macaroni and lasagne noodles.

Pasta is a delicious way to start a meal or to create a main meal. It can be served simply dressed with herbs and garlic, lemon juice, or a sauce of vegetables.

Observe the cooking time on the packet, use plenty of water for it to move around in and, when cooked, the pasta should be soft but still slightly bitey rather than claggy.

Brown rice or natural, has more protein, minerals and vitamins with fibre than processed white rice. The cooking time varies for brown rice, but it is nearly impossible to overcook it.

Rice has been a staple food in Asia for hundreds of years. Apart from serving rice to accompany many dishes, it easily creates a sumptuous meal served as a fried rice or cold mould.

almond rice ring

serves 4

1 cup cooked natural brown rice
1 bunch celery, leaves removed
½ cup grated onion
¾ cup chopped almonds
2 tbsps parsley finely chopped

2 tbsps basil finely chopped
1 tbsp plain wholemeal flour
4 egg whites
1½ cups skim milk
black pepper to taste

Pulp celery in a food processor. Squeeze out excess moisture and combine celery, onion, rice, almonds, parsley, basil and flour. Lightly beat egg whites and milk. Add to rice mixture. Pour into a mould. Place mould in a baking dish in a moderate oven for 30–40 minutes. When set unmould onto a serving plate. Serve with tomato sauce, a salad and wholemeal rolls.

chicken macaroni

serves 6

3 cups cooked wholemeal macaroni
2 cups chopped cooked chicken
1 tin tomatoes chopped and juice
1 cup celery chopped
1 cup green pepper chopped
1 cup grated carrot

¼ cup chopped chives
¼ cup chopped parsley
1 teaspoon fresh ginger grated (optional)
black pepper to taste
1 cup chicken or vegetable stock

Combine all ingredients in an oven proof dish. Cover and cook in a moderate oven for 30–40 minutes or until well heated through.

curried rice salad (hot)

serves 4–6

2 cups cold natural brown rice (cooked)
1 onion chopped
1 red pepper chopped
1 green pepper chopped
1 cup grated carrot

1 cup chopped celery
2 teaspoons fresh ginger grated
2 teaspoons curry powder (or to individual taste)
black pepper to taste

Combine all ingredients in a Chinese wok or frypan. Keep ingredients moving so they do not stick to the base of the pan. Cook for 4–5 minutes. Serve immediately.

raisin and walnut rice

serves 4–6

100g natural brown rice
pinch tumeric
50g chopped walnuts
1 teaspoon cummin seed

1½ tbsps coconut
½ cup raisins
¼ cup lemon juice

Boil rice in water and tumeric until cooked. Drain and leave to cool. Soak raisins in lemon juice until most of the juice has been absorbed. Drain off excess liquid.

In a heated Chinese wok, add rice, raisins, cummin seeds, walnuts and coconut. Stir fry 5 minutes or until heated through.

sweet and sour rice

serves 6–8

2 cups cold cooked natural brown rice
¼ cup unsweetened pineapple juice
1 teaspoon fresh ginger grated
1 onion chopped
1 cup raisins
1 cup chopped celery
1 cup red and green pepper chopped

1 cup carrot coarsely grated
1 cup pineapple chunks
½ cup chopped parsley
black pepper to taste
¼ teaspoon cummin (optional)
¼ cup sesame seeds or sunflower seeds (optional)

In a cold Chinese wok, add pineapple juice, ginger, onion and raisins. Turn on heat. When the liquid starts to boil, add all other ingredients and keep mixture moving. Cook for 5 minutes. Serve immediately.

tuna bake

1 large tin tuna in water, drained
3 cups cooked wholemeal macaroni
or natural brown rice
1 small can drained unsweetened
pineapple pieces
1 cup cooked corn kernels

1 cup chopped red and green pepper
2 shallots chopped
black pepper to taste
2 cups white sauce (see recipe in Sauces section)
1 cup wholemeal breadcrumbs
¼ cup low fat cheese

Combine tuna, macaroni or rice, pineapple, corn, pepper, shallots and black pepper. Pour over white sauce, sprinkle top with breadcrumbs and cheese. Bake in a hot oven until top is golden brown and tuna is heated through. Serve with a tossed salad.

vegetable fried rice

serves 5

2 cups cooked cold brown rice
1 small green pepper chopped finely
1 medium onion or 6 spring onions chopped
125g mushrooms sliced finely
1 medium carrot grated
1 cup bean shoots

1 cup finely shredded cabbage
black pepper to taste
¼ teaspoon chilli powder
2 egg whites
chopped parsley

Moisten the base of a non-stick pan or Chinese wok. Slowly cook egg whites until well set and chop up. Add rice and vegetables. Cook on low heat for 10 minutes. Keep moving the ingredients so rice and vegetables do not stick. Stir through parsley just prior to serving.

desserts

This section is especially reserved for those of us who are unable to accept a piece of fresh fruit as dessert at the conclusion of a meal.

apple and date cake

serves 8

Base:
1 cup wheatgerm
¼ cup coconut freshly grated
¼ cup almonds or sesame seeds
Filling:
8 medium granny smith apples

½ cup dates roughly chopped
1 teaspoon finely grated lemon rind
½–1 cup orange juice
Topping:
toasted muesli

Put the wheatgerm, coconut and almonds in a food processor and grind for 2 minutes. Line a 20cm round cake tin with foil. Press the wheatgerm mixture evenly over the base of the cake tin. Place in refrigerator until required.

Peel apples and slice thinly. Chop dates. Place in a saucepan with lemon rind and orange juice and gently cook until most of the moisture has been absorbed or until apples are tender. Pour off any excess liquid. Leave to cool just slightly.

Spoon the warm apple mixture over the wheatgerm and smooth down. Sprinkle toasted muesli over the top of apple evenly and press down with the palm of your hand.

Cook in a moderate oven for 30–40 minutes. Leave to cool. Refrigerate for at least 2 hours. The longer it is refrigerated, the easier it will be to remove it from the tin.

apricot buckwheat pancakes

2 cups S.R. wholemeal flour
1 teaspoon cinnamon
½ cup buckwheat

2 egg whites
enough skim milk to make a creamy batter

Place all ingredients in a blender and blend until smooth. Add ½ cup of milk at first and keep adding until desired consistency is obtained. Pour some mixture into a non-stick pancake skillet and cook until bubbles appear. Turn over and cook other side until just golden brown. Turn out. Repeat until all mixture has been used. Keep pancakes warm.

Apricot Filling:

500g fresh apricots halved and stones removed | *cottage cheese*
1 cup unsweetened orange juice | *toasted almonds or fresh apricot halves*
1 tbsp orange rind finely grated

Place apricots, orange juice and rind in a saucepan and gently simmer until tender and liquid has reduced and thickened. Chop apricots roughly. For a smoother filling, apricots could be put through a blender.

To serve, arrange layers of pancakes spread with cottage cheese, then pour over some of the apricot mixture until all pancakes have been used. Top with cottage cheese, some remaining apricot mixture and toasted almonds or fresh apricot halves.

Filling variations:
- substitute fresh peaches for the apricots
- mash bananas, add some orange juice, orange rind and 1 tbsp barley water
- apple puree, cinnamon and ½ cup raisins which have been softened by soaking in apple juice

barbecued fruits

For each person:

1 thinly sliced piece of pineapple
½ a fresh peach

Place fruit together on large skewers and turn slowly over very hot coals to heat through and barbecue slightly.

cassata

1 litre vanilla icecream (see recipe this section) | *½ cup chopped raisins*
1 cup chopped whole fresh almonds | *2 teaspoons brandy (optional)*
½ cup chopped washed glace cherries | *¼ cup toasted coconut*
1 cup mixed peel

Fold fruit and nut mixture into icecream prior to freezing icecream. Spoon into parfait glasses.

Chinese gooseberries, glazed

serves 4

4 large Chinese gooseberries well ripened | *2 tbsps brandy*
Sauce: | *2 large passionfruit*
3 tbsps apricot spread

Place sauce ingredients (apricot spread and brandy) in a small saucepan and heat through. Peel Chinese gooseberries and cut into slices. Overlap the slices on individual serving plates. Add passionfruit pulp to sauce and remove from heat. While still warm, spoon sauce over gooseberries evenly. Place the plates in the refrigerator until sufficiently chilled.

Serve alone or with a spoon of passionfruit icecream.

date and figballs with apple slices

makes approximately 30 balls

1 cup coconut
½ cup walnuts finely chopped
1 cup dates

250 g dried figs
1 teaspoon lemon juice
½ teaspoon lemon rind

Mince figs and dates and add coconut, lemon juice and lemon rind. Knead mixture well with your fingers. Roll into small balls and roll in finely chopped walnuts. Chill.

Serve these fruit balls with a bowl of apple slices, bunches of green grapes or chunks of pineapple.

date steamed pudding

1 cup chopped dates
1 cup sultanas
½ cup orange juice
1 teaspoon mixed spice

grated rind of 1 lemon
1 cup S. R. wholemeal flour
1 teaspoon bicarb of soda
½ cup skim milk combined with 1 dstsp vinegar

Place dates, sultanas, orange juice, mixed spice and lemon rind in a saucepan. Gently simmer for 3 minutes and remove. Leave to cool slightly.

Sift flour and bicarb of soda twice. Add flour to fruit mixture and stir in milk and vinegar.

Line a small pudding basin with foil. Pour in mixture. Seal tightly with foil and pudding basin lid. Place in a saucepan of boiling water and keep boiling for 1 hour.

fresh fruit and yoghurt

Serve platters of fresh fruit with bowls of yoghurt for dunking.

Variations:

Cinnamon Yoghurt
Add 2 heaped teaspoons of cinnamon to 1 cup of non-fat yoghurt and stir well.

Orange Yoghurt
Add 3 tbsps unsweetened orange juice and 1 tbsp finely grated orange rind.

fruit pudding, steamed

serves 4-6

½ cup currants
1 cup dried apricots
½ cup mixed peel
½ teaspoon ground cinmamon
⅛ teaspoon nutmeg

⅛ teaspoon ground cloves
½ cup orange juice
1 cup S.R. wholemeal stoneground flour
¼ cup skimmed milk
1 egg white beaten

Line a pudding basin with foil. Place fruits and spices and orange juice in a saucepan and let simmer for 5 minutes. Allow to cool but not to get cold. Sift flour and return husks. Add flour to fruit mixture, add milk and beaten egg white and stir well. Pour into pudding basin and cover tightly. Place in a large saucepan with boiling water. Steam pudding for 1-1½ hours. Do not let saucepan boil dry. Water in the saucepan should be boiling constantly. Serve with white sauce mixed with 2 teaspoons brandy (see recipe in Sauces section).

This pudding, when cold, could be refrigerated for 24 hours and cut into cake slices and served with coffee after a light chilled sweet or used as a fruit cake for morning or afternoon teas.

lemon mould with cherries

serves 4

500g ripe cherries
3 teaspoons gelatine
2 tbsps cold water
grated rind of 1 lemon

2 tbsps lemon juice
1 tbsp brandy
1 cup vanilla non-fat yoghurt
2 egg whites

Remove stones from cherries, wash and divide equally between 4 dessert dishes.

Place the gelatine into a cup or small bowl and mix with cold water. Stand this in a pan of hot water on a medium heat and leave until the gelatine has dissolved. Place the lemon rind and juice and brandy in a basin. Pour in the gelatine. Mix in the yoghurt and whisk. Whip the egg whites until soft peaks form and fold through the yoghurt mixture. Pour over the cherries. Place the dishes covered with plastic wrap into the refrigerator to set. It will take approximately 45 minutes. Decorate with fresh cherries.

This could be poured over any fresh fruit (kiwi fruit, strawberries, raspberries). It could be served plain with a platter of fresh fruits.

paw paw in passionfruit sauce

1 large paw paw
½ cup orange juice
3 large passionfruit

Remove seeds from paw paw. Peel away all the skin. Cut paw paw into chunky bite size pieces and place in a serving bowl. Combine orange juice and passionfruit pulp and pour over paw paw. Coat pieces of paw paw before chilling.

This refreshing dessert should be served well chilled.

peaches with a strawberry cream filling

serves 4

1 punnet strawberries
1 tbsp kirsch liqueur (optional)

¼ cup yoghurt
4 large fresh ripe peaches

Puree strawberries and add kirsch. Stir well. Fold in yoghurt. Refrigerate.

Carefully skin peaches. This can easily be done by placing a skewer or fork into peach and holding over a gas flame until the skin bursts (approx 1 or 2 minutes). Cut peaches in half, carefully scooping out the stone without damaging the peach halves. Place 2 peach halves on each serving plate and fill with strawberry cream. Chill until required.

pears in passionfruit sauce

serves 4

1½ cups orange juice
8 thin strips of orange rind
4 well ripened pears

¼ cup vanilla non-fat yoghurt
2 passionfruit

Place orange juice and rind in saucepan and heat. Peel pears and cut into 8 pieces. Gently place into the liquid and simmer for 10 minutes or until pears are tender. Turn the pears around in the liquid occasionally.

Add the yoghurt and boil rapidly until juices thicken somewhat. Remove from the heat and add passionfruit pulp. Place in a serving dish to cool slightly, but not to get cold.

pineapple, baked

serves 4

1 medium sized pineapple
1 teaspoon cinnamon

12 tbsps orange juice
2 tbsps orange rind

Cut pineapple in half lengthwise, cutting through the green top also. Then cut each half into two. Cut along the top of each quarter to remove the tough core which should come away easily in one long strip.

Wrap a piece of foil around the green top so it does not become brown while baking.

Place pineapple pieces, skin side down, on a foil lined baking tray. Cut wedges into each piece. Sprinkle cinnamon over pineapple quarters. Place in a moderate oven for 10 minutes or until pineapple is just warmed through.

Heat orange juice and rind and pour over pineapple just prior to serving.

pineapple and passionfruit mould

serves 8-10

1 litre of vanilla icecream (see recipe this section)
1 can drained crushed pineapple

pulp of 8 passionfruit

Fold through pineapple and passionfruit pulp prior to freezing icecream. Pour mixture into a mould and freeze.

To serve, quickly immerse mould into hot water for a few seconds. Turn mould onto a serving plate and decorate with pieces of fresh pineapple and bunches of grapes.

opposite:
birthday party: pizza (p 105); savoury jaffle surprise (p 106); kebab snacks (104); health chews (p 106); orange pineapple jelly (p 103); banana freeze with slices of fresh banana (p 102)
overleaf:
sunshine coast fruit salad (p 82)

pineapple tugboats

serves 4

2 large pineapples
3 oranges

3 pears (ripe)
6 passionfruit

Cut pineapples in half, including the greenery. Carefully cut away the pineapple flesh and cut into large bite size chunks. Peel oranges and segment. Peel and core pears and cut into large bite size chunks. Remove passionfruit pulp and add to the remaining fruit. Toss lightly so all fruits are coated with passionfruit. Spoon fruits into pineapple boats and chill well before serving.

Serve with home-made vanilla icecream or yoghurt.

platter of figs, grapes, walnuts and walnut and date balls

8 ripe fresh eating figs
green and purple grapes
walnuts in their shells

Walnut and Date Balls:
Soak 1 cup of chopped dates in orange juice for 1 hour. Drain and add ⅔ cup chopped walnuts. Roll into balls and roll in toasted coconut or toasted almonds and chill.

strawberry icecream cake

serves 8–10

1 litre of vanilla icecream (see recipe this section)
3 punnets of strawberries washed and hulled

½ cup toasted almond flakes
whole fresh strawberries for decoration

Make vanilla icecream, but do not freeze in the final step. Pour ⅓ of the icecream into a foil lined round tin. Slice strawberries finely and use half in a layer on top of the icecream mixture. Pour over ½ of remaining icecream mixture, another layer of strawberries, then the remaining icecream and freeze.

To serve, turn out of tin, remove foil and place on a serving plate. Sprinkle over toasted flaked almonds and decorate the edge of the strawberry cake with fresh whole strawberries.

strawberries in orange

2 punnets of strawberries
1 cup orange juice
1 tbsp brandy (optional)

Hull strawberries and puree approx a quarter of the quantity with the orange juice and brandy. Pour the orange liquid over remaining strawberries and chill well.

Serve plain or with a spoonful of orange yoghurt.

opposite:
strawberry ice cream cake (p 81)
previous page:
desserts: apple and date cake (p 76); fruit pudding steamed (p 79); baked pineapple (p 80)

sunshine coast fruit salad

Equal quantities of:

banana chunks	orange segments
apple chunks	strawberries
lemon juice	pineapple chunks
	3 kiwi fruit sliced

Squeeze lemon juice over banana and apple. Combine all the fruit and toss lightly. Chill well before serving.

The amount of fruit used will depend on the number of people eating the meal.

vanilla royale icecream

1 tin evaporated low fat milk	1 teaspoon vanilla
6 tbsps skim milk powder	4 egg whites
2 tbsps honey	

Combine the first four ingredients and beat until thick and creamy. Place in the freezer for 40 minutes. Remove from freezer and rebeat for 3 minutes. Beat egg whites until fluffy and peaks form. Fold egg whites through milk mixture. Pour into icecream trays and freeze.

winter fruit salad

serves 4-6

½ cup fresh dates halved and stoned	1 cup unsweetened orange juice
½ cup prunes halved and stoned	and 1 teaspoon cinnamon
½ cup dried figs, stalks removed and halved	½ cup seedless grapes
⅓ cup whole unblanched almonds	1 orange peeled and segmented
¼ cup walnut halves	2 small cantaloupes for serving (optional)

Combine dried fruits and nuts and place in a clean jar. Pour the liquid over them. Shake to coat the fruit with the liquid. Allow to soak for at least 4 hours. Can be stored for several weeks. Store in the refrigerator.

Remove small amount of flesh from cleaned and halved cantaloups. Spoon fruit mixture, leaving enough space to add grapes and orange segments into cantaloups.

Serve a bowl of home-made vanilla icecream to complement this salad. Eat the fruits and serve icecream in the cantaloup to absorb all the delicious juices that remain, or serve the icecream in goblets after the whole of the dessert has been eaten as a cool refreshment at the end of the meal.

yoghurt cheese pie

serves 8-10

Base:

½ cup wheatgerm	⅓ cup almonds finely ground

Combine and spread evenly over a foil-lined 20cm cake tin.

Filling:

1 cup plain non-fat yoghurt	1 teaspoon grated orange rind
250g cream cheese or cottage cheese	1 tbsp gelatine
2 tbsps honey	2 tbsps hot water
½ teaspoon vanilla	

Beat yoghurt, cream cheese, honey, vanilla and grated orange rind until smooth and creamy. Sprinkle gelatine over hot water and stir until dissolved. Let cool slightly. Fold through yoghurt mixture and pour over base. Refrigerate until firm. Sprinkle lightly with nutmeg. Cut into slices and serve. This pie will improve in flavour as it keeps.

cakes and breads

Cakes and bread are an important part of this diet. They are an excellent source of food fibre and add bulk that keeps the food moving through the system at the proper rate.

If you have been a connoisseur of the 'blow away' sponge and the Sunday Devonshire teas, you will need a little extra perseverance — but you and I both know the rewards are high.

apple cake

4 egg whites
¼ cup skim milk combined with
1 dessertspoon vinegar
1 teaspoon vanilla
125g minced dried apple (best done in a food processor)

175g cake flour or wholemeal S.R. flour
2 teaspoons baking powder
apple puree and passionfruit cream

Beat egg whites until stiff. Fold in milk and vinegar and vanilla. Add apple and carefully fold in. Sift cake flour and baking powder twice. Add to the egg white mixture and fold through gently until all flour is combined. Line a 20cm round cake tin with foil. Spoon mixture into cake tin. Bake in a moderate oven for 20 minutes. Turn out and cool.

Fillings:

Apple Filling

Cut cake into 3 layers and spread each layer with apple puree. Place cake in the refrigerator for 24 hours before cutting.

Passionfruit Cream and Apple Filling

Cut cake into 2 layers. Combine ½ cup cottage cheese and the pulp from 2 passionfruit. Beat well. Spread this mixture over the bottom layer of cake. Then top with apple puree. Place top layer on firmly and refrigerate the cake until required.

apple-rhubarb slice

Base:

1 cup wheatgerm
½ cup coconut

½ cup whole almonds
60g cottage cheese

Combine all ingredients in a food processor until well combined. Press mixture into a foil lined lamington tin.

Filling:

800g of apple and rhubarb stewed in
unsweetened orange juice and drained

2 teaspoons of lemon rind
1 teaspoon cinnamon

Spread apple, rhubarb mixture over base evenly.

Top:

Cover the top liberally with flaked almonds.

Cook in a moderately hot oven for three-quarters of an hour or until almonds are a golden brown. Cool and refrigerate. Cut into slices and serve.

apricot loaf

1 cup bran
1 cup chopped dried apricots
¾ cup mixed peel

2 cups skim milk
1½ cups wholemeal S.R. flour

Mix bran, apricots, mixed peel and milk in a bowl and let stand for 2 hours. Sift the flour and return husks. Add small amounts of flour and stir well until all ingredients are thoroughly mixed together. Put mixture into a non-stick loaf tin and bake in a moderate oven for about 1 hour.

bran fruit loaf

1 cup bran
1 cup chopped apricots
¾ cup raisins

1¾ cups skim milk
1½ cups wholemeal S.R. flour
extra bran

Mix bran, apricots, raisins and milk in a bowl and let stand for 2 hours. Sift the flour and return husks. Add small amounts of flour and stir well until all ingredients are thoroughly mixed. Lightly grease a loaf tin and place 2 tbsps bran in. Move bran around in the tin until the bottom and sides are well coated. Spoon cake mixture into tin. Sprinkle top of cake mixture with bran. Bake in a moderate oven for 1 hour or until cooked.

carrot loaf

2 cups wholemeal S.R. flour
1 teaspoon bicarb of soda
1 teaspoon nutmeg
1 cup chopped raisins
½ cup chopped walnuts

1½ cups grated carrot
2 egg whites
½ cup non fat yoghurt
1 cup skim milk

Sift flour, bicarb and nutmeg into a bowl. Return the husks. Stir in raisins, walnuts and carrot. Beat together eggs, yoghurt and milk. Pour into other ingredients and beat well. Cook in a slow oven for 1½ hours. Store in refrigerator for 2–3 days before cutting.

currant cake

1 cup bran
1 cup currants
¾ cup sultanas
2 cups skim milk

¼ cup chopped walnuts
1½ cups cake flour
3 teaspoons baking powder

Mix bran, currants, sultanas and milk in a bowl. Leave to stand for 2 hours. Sift the flour with the baking powder twice and incorporate with nuts. Add to the fruit and bran mixture. Beat well. Spoon into a non-stick loaf tin and bake in a moderate oven for 1 hour.

easy wholemeal bread

makes 3 loaves or 2 doz rolls or 6 French sticks

Basic Recipe:
60g compressed yeast
800ml warm water
400ml warm skim milk
5 metricups unbleached white bread flour
5 metricups wholemeal flour

Combine yeast, water and milk. Stir to dissolve yeast. Sift flours into a large bowl. Make a well in the centre and pour in yeast mixture. Move flour from sides of the bowl and sprinkle lightly over yeast. Leave in a warm place for approximately 20 minutes to allow the yeast to sponge. Mix thoroughly with a long straight edged knife or spatula until all the flour is absorbed. The mixture should be quite tacky. Flour the bench very well and empty dough onto it. It will be very sticky, so continue to use the knife or spatula and turn dough over from the sides to the centre until the dough is completely covered in flour. Place in a clean bowl and set aside to rise. Leave for approximately 40 minutes to 1 hour. When dough has risen approximately 5cm empty out again onto a well floured board or bench and lightly turn dough over — outside edges to the centre. Turn dough over and shape loaves, rolls, or French sticks.

For Loaves:
Cut into six equal parts to make three high tin loaves. Place 2 parts in each tin and set aside for dough to double in size or to reach the top of the tin. Wipe the top with water or skim milk. Sprinkle over with poppy seeds, caraway seeds, cracked wheat, rolled oats, wheat flakes or fresh herbs.

For Rolls:
Take small pieces of dough, roll out like a sausage and tie in a knot. Top as for loaves. Place them side by side. Cook at 350 degrees F (180 degrees C) for 25–30 minutes.

For French Sticks:
Divide dough into six equal parts. Roll each part out like a sausage. These sticks will rise nicely if cooked in a proper French stick tin. Top as for loaves and with a knife make slits along the top of sticks. Cook at 350 degrees F (180 degrees C) for 20–25 minutes.

Variations:
Herb Bread:
Add 2 tablespoons or more of your favourite fresh herb finely chopped, e.g. parsley, chives, oregano, basil.

Garlic Bread:
Add 1 tablespoon or more of garlic powder.

Onion Bread:
Add 1 tablespoon or more of onion powder or dried onion flakes.

Sweet Bread:
Add 2 tablespoons or more finely chopped lemon rind, orange rind or mandarine rind.

Spiced Fruit Bread:
Add 2 teaspoons mixed spice and 1 teaspoon cinnamon and add 1 cup finely minced, mixed dried fruit.

Grain Bread:

Add ½ cup cracked wheat, ½ cup rye grain, ¼ cup rolled oats. Add more water if dough becomes too dry.

Oatmeal Bread:

Add 1 cup rolled oats. Add more water or skim milk if dough becomes too dry.

fruity pumpkin cake

1 cup mashed cold pumpkin
125g sultanas
125g raisins
125g mixed dried peel
125g finely chopped dried apricots
1 tbsp honey
1 cup unsweetened orange or *apple juice*
1 teaspoon bicarb of soda

4 egg whites
250g wholemeal S.R. flour
1 teaspoon mixed spice

Combine fruit, orange juice (2 teaspoons of brandy for special occasions) and honey in a saucepan. Bring to the boil. Remove from heat. Add bicarb of soda. Cool. Grease a 20cm round tin very lightly or line with foil.

Heat oven to 325 degrees F (165 degrees C). Beat egg whites lightly. Add cold pumpkin and fruit mixture and beat until smooth. Stir in flour and spice and beat until smooth. Bake for 1½ hours.

For a more moist cake, soak fruit in orange juice overnight.

moist mandarine and banana cake

125g cottage cheese
1 cup dates
peel from ½ a mandarine (remove pith)
4 egg whites
3 very ripe bananas or 1 banana and 2 grated apples

1 teaspoon vanilla
2 tbsp chopped walnuts (optional)
1½ cups wholemeal S.R. flour
1 teaspoon bicarb of soda

Mash bananas. Place dates and mandarine peel in a food processor and mince finely. Cream cottage cheese and date mixture until quite smooth. Beat in 1 egg white at a time. Add bananas and vanilla then walnuts. Sift flour and bicarb of soda and fold through gently. Cook in a 20cm ring tin or a 20cm deep fluted tin at 350 degrees F (180 degrees C) for 35–40 minutes.

Variation
Apricot Tea Cakes:
Makes approximately 30. Substitute ¾ cup apricot pulp for bananas. Omit mandarine peel. Spoon mixture into paper patty pans. Cook at 350 degrees F (180 degrees C) for 15–20 mins.

Note:
This is a very versatile cake recipe, that you could substitute any fruit or fruit combination. The quantity should be ¾ cup. You could substitute mandarine peel for orange or lemon peel.

opposite:
cakes: apple cake (p 84); moist mandarine and banana cake (p 88); small apricot tea cakes (p 85); fruity pumpkin cake (p 87); sesame scone roll (p 90)
overleaf:
1   lunch box suggestions: chicken box, celery and crackers (p 105)
2   breads and spreads: easy wholemeal bread loaves and rolls (p 86); apple spread (p 116); plum spread (p 117); apricot fruit spread (p 116)
3   the health sandwich (p 104)

muesli loaf

2 cups wholemeal S.R. flour
1 teaspoon mixed spice
30g non fat yoghurt
1 cup sugar free toasted muesli

½ cup chopped raisins
1 cup grated raw carrot
1 egg white unbeaten
1 cup skim milk

Sift the flour with the mixed spice, return husks to the bowl. Add yoghurt and mix well. Add toasted muesli, raisins and carrot. Mix well. Add egg white and milk and beat well until all ingredients are combined. Turn into a non-stick 25x10cm loaf tin. Bake in a moderate oven for 1 hour.

no bake festive cake

9 cups wholewheat cereal crushed
375g prunes
apple juice
125g dates chopped
155g raisins chopped
90g walnuts
2 teaspoons grated orange rind

1 teaspoon grated lemon rind
¾ cup sultanas or apricots or dried apple
½ teaspoon cinnamon
½ teaspoon ginger
½ cup unsweetened orange juice
2 teaspoons brandy or rum (optional)

Cook prunes in enough apple juice to cover until tender and drain well. Chop prunes finely. Crush cereal and add to prunes with all other ingredients and mix well. Pack mixture into a 20cm foil lined cake tin and cover with foil.

Refrigerate for at least 3 days before cutting. Decorate the top of the cake with blanched whole almonds and cut into thin slices to serve.

savoury bread loaf

½ cup buckwheat
8-10 slices wholemeal bread, crumbed
1 grated carrot
1 cup finely chopped celery
1 small onion finely chopped

2 small apples grated
½ cup finely chopped red pepper
2 tbsps date and apple chutney
1 egg white
black pepper to taste

Combine all ingredients and mix well. Press into a loaf tin and bake in a water dish for 30 minutes or until firm in a moderate oven. Remove from oven and let cool in tin. Turn out and refrigerate.

This can be sliced and used as a substitute for meat served with a salad, served plain or served as slices on dry crackers topped with a slice of tomato and a pepper ring.

sesame fruit loaf

1 cup All Bran
1 cup skim milk
1 cup wheatgerm
1 teaspoon bicarb of soda
½ cup sultanas

½ cup currants
½ cup raisins
½ cup chopped walnuts
1 tbsp honey or golden syrup
toasted sesame seeds

Soak bran in milk for 5 minutes. Then add all other ingredients and mix thoroughly. Spoon into a foil lined loaf tin. Sprinkle with toasted sesame seeds. Bake in a moderate oven for 35–40 minutes.

sesame scone roll

2 cups stoneground wholemeal S.R. flour
½ cup non fat yoghurt

¾ cup skim milk
1 dessertspoon lemon juice

Place flour and yoghurt in a food processor and blend until mixture resembles fine breadcrumbs. Combine lemon juice and skim milk. Make a well in the flour and yoghurt mixture and pour in milk and lemon juice. Knead mixture on a lightly floured board and roll out to 2cm thickness.

Filling:

1 medium onion grated
1 carrot grated
1 green pepper grated
1 large potato grated

1 tbsp tabbouleh
1 tbsp parsley finely chopped
1 tbsp mint finely chopped
½ teaspoon dry basil

Blend all ingredients together. Spread over scone mixture and roll up. Dampen the top of scone roll with yoghurt and sprinkle with sesame seeds. Bake in a hot oven (400 degrees F, 200 degrees C) for half an hour or until nicely browned. Slice and serve.

Variation:

Cook for 25 minutes. Remove from oven. Cut into 5cm slices and form the slices in a circle. Sprinkle over finely grated low fat cheese. Serve with a salad in the centre.

pastry

These two pastry recipes should not be likened to puff pastry or shortcrust pastry. They are both a casing for pies or pasties and add roughage to the diet. They should be cooked at a low to moderate temperature until filling is cooked and pastry is just lightly browned. If cooked in a very hot oven, the pastry becomes quite brittle.

The quantity is enough to line and top a 20cm pie dish or line a large pie dish, and makes approximately six average size pasties.

wheatgerm pastry

180g wholemeal plain flour
60g wheatgerm

90g cottage cheese
1tbsp lemon juice

Combine all ingredients (preferably in a food processor) until mixture becomes a smooth ball. Knead lightly on a floured board and roll out to required size. If using this pastry to line a pie dish, use a fork to make air holes in base and sides of pastry case.

wholemeal potato pastry

250g wholemeal plain flour sifted
1 medium potato, peeled and finely grated

⅓ cup water
3 tbsps lemon juice

Combine all ingredients (preferably in a food processor) until mixture becomes a smooth ball. Knead lightly on a floured board and roll out to required size. Leave pastry to rest while preparing filling.

breakfasts

cinnamon pears

serves 4

4 pears
1½ cups apple juice, unsweetened

rind of 1 lemon
½ teaspoon cinnamon

Peel whole pears and leave stems on. Stand pears up in a saucepan. Pour over apple juice, lemon rind and cinnamon. Place lid on saucepan and simmer over very gentle heat until just tender. Serve warm.

home made toasted muesli and fresh fruit

makes approx. 6 cups
allow ½ cup home made toasted muesli and a piece of fresh fruit per person

1 cup wheat flakes
2 cups rolled oats
1½ cups unprocessed bran
½ cup raw coconut
½ cup wheat germ (optional)
¼ cup skim milk powder

60g sultanas
60g currants
60g raisins
60g finely cut dried apricots
60g finely cut dried peaches

Place the first four ingredients on a large baking tray. Spread out evenly. Place in a very hot oven for 5–10 minutes or until browning occurs. Turn over once and leave for a further 3–5 minutes. Do not burn. Remove from oven and spread out on paper to cool.

When completely cool, place in a container with remaining ingredients and mix well. Make sure the container is well sealed.

Fresh Fruit
Sliced banana, peach or pear would be an excellent choice in fresh fruit.

orange grapefruit

serves 1
½ grapefruit
1 slice of an orange

Place the slice of orange on top of the grapefruit. Cover with plastic wrap and refrigerate overnight. This procedure allows the natural sweetness of the grapefruit and orange to combine and give a very sweet fruit.

To serve cut a slit in the slice of orange from its centre to the outside and twist to stand orange up on grapefruit.

Serve with a cup of hot lemon water (cup of hot water and a slice of lemon).

pineapple island floats
serves 2

1 small ripe pineapple
cooked apple

Cut pineapple in half, keeping the leaves on. Carefully remove pineapple flesh without damaging the shell. Cut pineapple into bite size chunks. Refrigerate.

Cooked Apple

2 large granny smith apples   *lemon rind*
½ lemon   *1 teaspoon cinnamon*
½ cup apple juice

Peel and core apples. Slice thinly. Place in a saucepan and add remaining ingredients. Place lid on saucepan and simmer gently over low heat until apples are tender. Drain. Keep any juice. Serve warm apple on one side of half pineapple shell and chunks of pineapple on the other side.

porridge
serves 2

1 cup rolled oats   *2 teaspoons lemon rind*
¼ cup unprocessed bran   *2 teaspoons orange rind*
2½ cups water   *cinnamon to taste*

Combine rolled oats and unprocessed bran in a saucepan with the cold water. Slowly bring to the boil. Add remaining ingredients and cook gently for 5 minutes.

Serve with fresh fruit and skim milk.

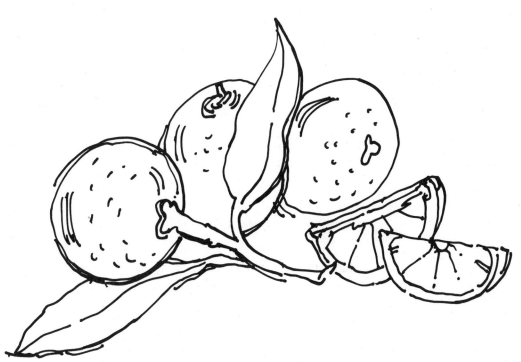

rice and fruit

serves 1

½ cup cooked natural brown rice   *cooked apricots or*

¼ cup skim milk   *choice of fresh or other cooked fruit*

If you always keep a container of cooked natural brown rice in the refrigerator, this breakfast idea is effortless.

If cooking rice for a number of people, allow ¼ cup per person. Boil until cooked. Drain and run under cold water to cool. Leave to drain.

Cooked Apricots

apricots   *orange rind*

orange juice

Allow 2–3 whole apricots per person. Wash apricots and place in saucepan. Cover the base of saucepan with unsweetened orange juice. Add grated orange rind. Place lid on saucepan and simmer over very gentle heat until just tender.

Serve cooked apricots on cold rice with skim milk and freshly squeezed juice of a chilled orange.

tangy canteloupe

serves 2

1 small canteloupe   *½ cup unsweetened orange juice*

rind of 1 small orange and lemon

Cut canteloupe in half. Remove seeds and leave to stand. Place orange juice, orange and lemon rind in a saucepan. Simmer over very gentle heat for 3 minutes. Remove from heat and let cool. Pour equal quantities of the orange liquid into each half of the canteloupe. Carefully cover with plastic wrap. Refrigerate for at least 24 hours before serving. Remove plastic wrap and serve.

A spoonful of natural non-fat yoghurt would be an excellent addition.

wholemeal rolls with spreads

serves 4

a basket of hot wholemeal rolls — allow 1–2 rolls per person (see recipe in Breads section)

cottage cheese

selection of spreads (see recipe in Sauces & Dressings section)

Open rolls. Spread with cottage cheese and spread of your choice. Serve with glass of fresh chilled orange juice or apple juice.

yoghurt pots

serves 1

1 cup natural non-fat yoghurt   *2 tbsps suitable spread*

¼ cup cooked fruit (apples, pears, plums, rhubarb, apricots) *½ teaspoon vanilla*

Choose a container (preferably ceramic as it retains a perfect chilled temperature) that is at least 1 cup capacity and has a lid.

Place your desired ¼ cup of cooked fruit on the base of the pot. Combine yoghurt, spread of your choice and vanilla. Lightly stir. Pour over fruit. Place lid on top. Keep in refrigerator for at least 24 hours to let flavours blend. Remove lid and serve in the pot.

breakfast: orange grapefruit (p 14) sweet jaffle surprise (banana & raisin) (p 106)

drinks: pineapple milk shake (p 100); apple milk shake (p 98); fruit cup (p 99); summer party punch (p 100)

drinks

apple milk drink

serves 2
1 cup apple juice well chilled   *sprinkle of cinnamon on top*
1 cup skim milk well chilled
Blend until thick and foamy.

apricot and vanilla drink

serves 1

1 cup skim milk   *1 teaspoon vanilla*
4 fresh apricots stoned
Blend thoroughly until thick and foamy.

banana milk

serves 1
1 cup skim milk   *1 teaspoon brewer's yeast*
1 mashed banana   *sprinkle of nutmeg on top*
2 teaspoons skim milk powder
Place all ingredients in a blender.

barley water

3 tbsps pearl barley
enough water to cover
9 additional cups water

juice and peel of 2 oranges
juice and peel of 2 lemons
1 tbsp honey

Cover barley with water. Bring to the boil, strain and discard water. Cover barley with 9 cups of water, bring to the boil and simmer for 15 minutes.

In a large jug, add honey, juice and peel of oranges and lemons. Pour barley water in through a sieve. Discard barley. Leave to cool. Remove peel and refrigerate.

This is an excellent thirst quencher or a pick-me-up if you're not feeling well.

fruit and vegetable cocktails

½ cup well chilled water
Add one of the following combinations and place in a food processor or juice extractor. Strain and pour into a glass. Garnish with ice blocks, a slice of lemon or orange, mint, parsley, cucumber peel, cherries, strawberries.

Combinations:
1 apple, 1 peeled carrot, 1 stick of celery
2 peeled carrots, ¼ lemon peeled and pith removed, parsley sprigs
1 apple, 1 stick rhubarb, 1 orange peeled and pith removed
3 slices fresh pineapple, 1 carrot, 1 small wedge of lemon
1 grapefruit peeled and pith removed, 2 slices of fresh pineapple
2 apples, sprig of mint
1 orange peeled and pith removed, ¼ lemon peeled and pith removed, sprig of mint
Try topping up with soda water for a variation.

fruit cup

Equal quantities of:
orange juice
apple juice

pineapple juice
½ passionfruit pulp

Combine equal quantities of orange juice, apple juice and pineapple juice. Stir through ½ cup passionfruit pulp for every 2 litres of combined juice. Add ice blocks and dilute with water, mineral water or soda water.

island thirst quencher

125ml non fat yoghurt
125ml unsweetened pineapple juice
¼ cup crushed pineapple drained
Blend all ingredients and garnish with chopped mint and top up with soda water.

orange milk

serves 1

1 cup orange juice

2 teaspoons skim milk powder

¼ teaspoon vanilla

1 tbsp icecream

Place all ingredients in a blender

pineapple milk shake

1 cup well chilled skim milk

¾ cup well chilled pineapple juice

2 teaspoons skim milk powder or 1 tbsp icecream

mint to garnish

Blend thoroughly until thick and foamy.

summer party punch

serves 10–14

1 litre orange juice

500ml unsweetened pineapple juice

500g strawberries pureed

1½ litres soda water

ice blocks

Combine orange juice, pineapple juice, strawberries and chill well. Add soda water and iceblocks prior to serving. Garnish each glass with a fruit kebab.

Fruit Kebabs:

cocktail sticks

cubes of green skinned apple

pineapple chunks

strawberries

Thread fruit onto cocktail sticks and place one in each glass.

just for kids

If we fail to grab children's attention when they are young, and give them a basic education on the desirable foods, then we will surely lose them in their fight for a healthy being.

apricot nibbles

makes 20

¾ cup dried apricots
¾ cup coconut
1 level teaspoon grated lemon rind

1 level teaspoon grated orange rind
1 tbsp orange juice
toasted coconut

Cover apricots with boiling water and let stand for 10 minutes to soften. Drain.

   Mince or finely chop the apricots and mix in the coconut. Add remaining ingredients, knead until well blended. If mixture is too dry, add more orange juice; if too wet, add more coconut. Shape into small balls and roll in toasted coconut.

banana freeze

2 cups plain non-fat yoghurt
2 teaspoons lemon juice
½ cup orange juice
1 tbsp orange or lemon rind

¼ cup honey
2 egg whites
2 mashed bananas

Blend together the first five ingredients and pour into an icecream tray. Freeze until mixture starts to set. Remove from icecream tray and beat until smooth. Beat egg whites until stiff and fold through ice mixture alternately with mashed bananas. Pour into icecream trays and freeze. Serve with fresh bananas.

banana pikelets

makes 12

1 cup wholemeal flour
1 small banana mashed
squeeze of lemon juice

1 teaspoon grated lemon rind
enough skim milk to make
a dropping consistency batter

Combine all ingredients and stir in milk. Heat a non-stick skillet and drop spoonfuls of the mixture onto it. As bubbles appear on top of each pikelet, turn over so the bottoms brown. Remove from pan and continue until all the mixture is used. Serve topped with slices of fresh banana.

fish and chips

fish fillets
wholemeal flour
fine wholemeal breadcrumbs
egg white

lemon juice
potatoes cut into chips
natural non-fat yoghurt

Squeeze lemon juice over the fish. Dip fish in flour and shake off excess. Dip in egg white and press down in breadcrumbs until both sides are evenly coated. Shake off any excess. Refrigerate fish in crumbs for at least 2 hours prior to cooking. Cook in a non-stick pan until both sides are golden brown. Do not overcook.

Lightly boil potato chips until tender but not too soft. Drain. Place on a non-stick baking tray and wipe over with natural non-fat yoghurt. Bake in a hot oven approx 10-15 minutes until golden brown.

fruit pikelets

makes 12
1 cup wholemeal flour
½ cup raisins, sultanas, mixed peel
1 teaspoon grated lemon or orange rind when using raisins or sultanas
enough skim milk to make a dropping consistency batter

Combine all ingredients and stir in milk. Heat a non-stick skillet and drop spoonfuls of the mixture onto it. As bubbles appear on top of each pikelet, turn over so the bottoms brown. Remove from pan and continue until all the mixture is used.

health chews, apricot and almond

½ cup chopped dried apricots
¼ cup orange juice
2 tbsps honey
½ cup skim milk powder
¼ cup whole almonds chopped roughly

1 tbsp toasted sesame seeds
1 teaspoon grated orange rind
½ cup sultanas or currants
¼ cup coconut
extra raw toasted coconut

Place apricots, orange juice and honey in a saucepan and simmer over low heat for 10 minutes or until apricots are tender. Do not drain. Blend in skim milk powder, add almonds, sesame seeds, grated orange rind, sultanas and coconut. Mix well and leave to cool slightly.

Roll mixture into a log shape and roll in toasted coconut. Roll up in foil and keep in refrigerator.

Cut into slices and store in a jar or wrap each individual piece in foil and different coloured cellophane and present as a gift which will be enjoyed immensely.

health sandwich

serves 1
3 slices of wholemeal bread
chicken salad ·
Spread 1 piece of bread with date and apple chutney. Spread over chopped cooked chicken. Season with black pepper to taste. Top with second piece of bread. Spread with cottage cheese, slices of tomato, beetroot slices, onion slices, cucumber slices, alfalfa sprouts and season with black pepper, chopped chives or chopped parsley. Top with third piece of bread.

Variations:
Beef Coleslaw
Spread 1 piece of bread with Dijon mustard and add a slice of rare beef. Season with black pepper to taste. Top with second piece of bread. Spread with cottage cheese, slices of tomato, cucumber, onion and a large lettuce leaf. Season with black pepper. Top with third piece of bread.

Salad Combination
Spread 1 piece of bread with mayonnaise and add a lettuce leaf, slices of tomato, cucumber, alfalfa sprouts. Season with black pepper. Top with second slice of bread. Spread with mayonnaise, slices of beetroot, grated carrot, chopped celery and finish with another lettuce leaf. Season with black pepper and top with the third piece of bread.

icypoles, homemade

- *apple juice (unsweetened)*
- *orange juice diluted with water (unsweetened)*
- *orange juice and passionfruit pulp*
- *pineapple juice (unsweetened) with crushed pineapple pieces*

Pour ingredients into plastic icypole moulds and freeze.

icypoles, creamy

- skim milk, bananas and lemon juice (blend all ingredients)
- skim milk, apple juice (blend equal quantities together)
- mixed chopped fresh fruit (e.g. oranges, apple, pineapple, passionfruit, mango, cantaloupe) and non-fat yoghurt (blend equal quantities together)

Pour ingredients into plastic icypole moulds and freeze.

kebab snacks

1 wooden skewer per person	*pineapple wedges*
cheese chunks	*grapes*
celery chunks	*radish chunks*
carrot chunks	*tomato chunks*

Thread variations of these ingredients onto a skewer and make a great in-between mealtime snack or prelude to a main meal.

lunch box ideas

Chicken Box

steamed chicken drumsticks

wholemeal roll

1 tomato

lettuce

container of non-fat yoghurt and corn

Celery and Crackers

container of cottage cheese, chopped celery, chopped chicken, chopped walnuts, shredded lettuce

wholewheat grain crackers

sticks of celery

Salad Box

wholemeal roll

1 tomato

1 apple cucumber

½ small lettuce heart

chunks of low-fat cheese

sticks of celery

Fruit Box

container of cottage cheese or non-fat yoghurt

1 apple

1 orange

chunks of pineapple

1 banana

orange pineapple jelly

serves 6

¼ litre boiling water

¼ litre unsweetened orange juice

3 teaspoons gelatine

1 teaspoon grated lemon rind

1 cup crushed unsweetened pineapple

Dissolve gelatine in ¼ litre boiling water. Stir in orange juice and grated lemon rind. As jelly is nearly setting, fold through pineapple. Refrigerate until set. Serve with vanilla icecream or non-fat yoghurt.

pizza

Base:

wholemeal peta bread

Sauce:

1 onion

1 clove garlic

2 carrots grated

1 tin tomatoes and juice

1 tbsp tomato paste

black pepper to taste

Puree all the ingredients and slowly bring to the boil. Simmer for 5 minutes. Cool slightly. Spread over peta bread and top with ricotta cheese, sliced tomatoes, sliced capsicum, sliced mushrooms and crushed unsweetened pineapple. Bake in a very hot oven for 10-15 minutes. Serve with a salad.

raisin puffs

makes 24

2 cups soy flour

4 teaspoons baking powder

1 cup chopped raisins

2 teaspoons orange or lemon rind

1 dessertspoon of honey or golden syrup

1-1½ cup skimmed milk

60g finely minced dried apple

Sift flour and baking powder together twice. Add raisins, rind, honey or golden syrup. Stir, adding the milk. Mixture should be slightly sticky. Add apples. Place teaspoons of mixture into paper patties and place on a baking tray. Bake in a moderate oven for 15 minutes or until tops are golden brown. Break open and fill with apple spread or apricot and fruit spread.

savoury jaffle surprise

serves 1

2 slices of wholemeal bread
ricotta cheese or *date and apple chutney* or *tomato relish*
Spread one or both slices with any one of the above and add any of the following:

- grated carrot, chopped celery and sliced tomato.
- sliced tomato and low-fat cheese slices.
- leftover fish, flaked with chopped chives.
- leftover chicken, thinly sliced pineapple.
- leftover curried vegetables
- grated carrot, low-fat cheese slices, raisins

sweet jaffle surprise

serves 1
2 slices of wholemeal bread
cottage cheese
Spread one or both slices of bread with cottage cheese and add any of the following:

- mashed or sliced banana and raisins.
- thinly sliced apple, lemon juice and chopped dates
- apple spread and sultanas.
- apple spread, grated apple and cinnamon.
- apricot and fruit spread, finely chopped walnuts.

savoury pikelets

makes 12

¼ teaspoon bicarb soda
1 egg white
⅔ cup skim milk
1 cup wholemeal S.R. flour

½ teaspoon curry
½ teaspoon mustard
1 teaspoon wine or herb vinegar
grated low-fat cheese

Add egg white, milk and vinegar to dry ingredients and mix well. Add cheese and fold through. Drop spoonfuls onto a non-stick pan and cook until both sides are brown. Top with slices of tomato.

vanilla icecream

makes 3-4 litres

1 can low fat evaporated milk well chilled
6 tbsps skim milk powder
1 cup non-fat yoghurt
2 tbsps honey
½ teaspoon vanilla
Combine all ingredients in a large bowl and beat for 3 minutes. Place in the freezer for 40 minutes until well chilled and starting to ice up. Remove from freezer and beat until creamy, thick and double in size. Pour into icecream trays and freeze.

dressings

A dressing can enhance the flavour of the salad ingredients without necessarily adding oil.

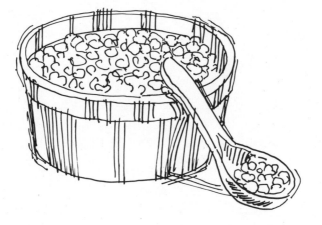

cottage cheese

makes 1½ cups

1 plain junket tablet

1 tbsp water

4 cups skim milk

Crush the junket tablet with the back of a spoon in a large bowl and dissolve in water. Warm the milk to lukewarm. Pour the milk over the dissolved junket tablet and stir to combine. Allow to stand in a warm place until set. Cut through the curd into rough pieces. Place a sheet of muslin over a strainer and pour the junket into it. Gather up the corners of the cloth and tie securely. Allow to stand over the strainer in a cool place for a few hours or overnight to allow the whey to drain. When the curd is beginning to firm, place into an airtight container. Cover and store in the refrigerator. This will keep for at least 4 days.

creamy cucumber dressing

½ cup non fat yoghurt

¼ teaspoon dry dill

4 teaspoons fresh lemon juice

½ cup coarsely grated peeled cucumber

ground black pepper to taste

Combine all ingredients and chill. This could also be used as a dip to serve with a platter of raw vegetables.

cucumber dressing

1 cup non fat yoghurt

½ small seeded cucumber grated

2 tbsps chopped parsley

2 tbsps chopped chives

1 tbsp lemon juice

1 tbsp vinegar

Combine all ingredients and chill.

French dressing

2 tbsps fresh basil or 1 tsp dry
½ teaspoon pepper
⅓ cup fresh lemon juice

2 tbsps fresh parsley
2 teaspoons fresh lemon rind
⅔ cup wine vinegar

Place all ingredients in a sealed jar. Shake well and store in the refrigerator.

fruity dressing

1 cup unsweetened orange juice
½ cup lemon vinegar
½ cucumber peeled and seeded
2 cloves garlic

1 tbsp lemon rind grated
1 tbsp orange rind grated
2 tbsps chopped fresh herbs
(parsley, basil, chives, thyme)

Combine all ingredients except lemon and orange rind and fresh herbs. Blend in a food processor for 1 minute. Add other ingredients but do not blend. Shake well and store in sealed jars in the refrigerator.

garlic dressing

1 cup vinegar
½ cup water
juice of 1 lemon

½ cucumber peeled and seeded
2–3 cloves garlic
black pepper to taste

Combine all ingredients in a food processor and blend for 1 minute. Place in sealed jars and store in the refrigerator.

home style yoghurt (1)

1 litre skim milk
4 tbsps skim milk powder

2 tbsps commercial natural yoghurt

Pour milk into saucepan, add milk powder and stir until dissolved. Heat milk gently until it reaches boiling point. Cool until tepid.

Blend a little milk into the yoghurt until smooth, then stir thoroughly into remaining milk. Pour mixture into a sterilised wide-mouthed vacuum flask, cover and stand for 4–6 hours, by which time it should set to a firm yoghurt. Do not disturb until yoghurt has set. Refrigerate.

Tips:

1   It is best to start yoghurt making using fresh commercial yoghurt (under 7 days)
2   Adding the yoghurt to milk hotter than 45 degrees will destroy the bacterial culture and prevent the setting action.
3   Add any flavourings to yoghurt once it has set and before refrigerating.

home style yoghurt (2)

1½ cups skim milk powder
600ml hot water

3 tbsps commercial yoghurt

Put skim milk powder in basin and make a well in the centre. Gradually stir in water and whisk until milk powder has dissolved. Take ½ cup of this milk and blend in a cup with yoghurt. Add to the remaining milk and stir well. Pour into a sterilised wide-mouthed vacuum flask, cover and stand for 4–6 hours, by which time it should set to a firm yoghurt. Do not disturb until yoghurt has set. Refrigerate.

island dressing

½ cup non fat yoghurt
½ cup ricotta cheese
juice of 1 lemon
⅓ cup tomato puree

3 drops tabasco sauce
3 teaspoons chopped green pepper
finely chopped parsley
finely chopped chives

Put all ingredients except parsley and chives in blender and process till smooth. Fold through parsley and chives and store in the refrigerator.

mixed herb dressing

1 cup herb vinegar
1 cup apple juice
juice of 1 lemon

½ cucumber peeled and seeded
2 tbsps mixed herbs (parsley, chives, thyme, dill)

Combine the first four ingredients in a food processor and blend for 1 minute. Add herbs but do not blend. Place in sealed jars and store in the refrigerator.

ricotta cheese

makes approximately 2 cups
4½ litres skim milk
⅓ cup fresh lemon juice

Scald the milk then remove it from the heat. Stir the lemon juice into the milk. Let it sit for at least 20 minutes. Strain to remove the liquid (whey) from the curds, pressing the curds to remove as much liquid as possible. Chill.

sour cream

½ cup non fat yoghurt
½ cup ricotta cheese

squeeze of lemon juice
black pepper

Combine all ingredients in a blender until smooth then store in the refrigerator.

tarragon vinegar

1 cup tarragon leaves picked just before flowering and washed well
5 cups white wine vinegar

Place tarragon leaves in a jar and pour over vinegar. Cover and allow to stand 2–3 weeks. Shake frequently. Strain and pour into sterilised jars. Place a sprig of tarragon in each jar and seal. Use as required.

Variations:

Herb Vinegar

Substitute tarragon leaves with 1 tbsp each of chopped chives, marjoram, basil and parsley.

Lemon or Orange Vinegar

Substitute tarragon leaves with thinly peeled rind of 2 oranges or 2 lemons.

sauces

custard

makes 1 cup

1 cup of white sauce (omit black pepper). Add the juice from ½ an orange, the rind of 1 orange finely grated and 1 teaspoon of vanilla. Beat well.

date sauce (cold)

500g dates finely chopped
1 cup unsweetened orange juice

1 tbsp orange rind finely grated
1 cup non fat yoghurt

Bring dates to the boil in orange juice and let simmer for 10 minutes or until dates are tender. Let cool. Puree dates and fold through yoghurt when cool. Refrigerate. Serve date sauce with a platter of vegetables.

gravy

serves 4

2 tbsps wholemeal plain flour
½ cup chicken stock, water or
juice from the meat you're cooking

½ cup vegetable juice
½ cup water or dry white wine
black pepper to taste

Brown the flour in a saucepan or pan over low heat. Remove from heat and cool slightly. Add the stock and beat to a smooth paste. Slowly add the vegetable juice, water or wine, stirring constantly. Add black pepper to taste. Let simmer gently for 2 minutes and serve, or,

Brown the flour, add all the other ingredients and blend them in a food processor. Blend for 1 minute. Return to the saucepan. Cook for 5 minutes or until gravy has thickened.

herb sauce

1 cup non fat yoghurt
1 teaspoon Dijon mustard
1½ tbsps white wine vinegar
½ tbsp lemon juice

black pepper
1 tbsp chopped chives
1 tbsp chopped dill
1 tbsp chopped parsley

Combine yoghurt, mustard, vinegar, lemon juice and black pepper in a blender or shake thoroughly in a jar. Fold through chives, dill and parsley.

mayonnaise

1 cup plain non fat yoghurt
2 teaspoons lemon juice
1 teaspoon dry mustard

½ teaspoon paprika
freshly ground black pepper

Mix all ingredients together and shake well. Keep in the refrigerator and use as needed.

mushroom sauce (hot)

1kg mushrooms peeled and sliced
¼ cup water

cornflour to thicken

Place mushrooms in a saucepan with ¼ cup water. Let simmer very gently with a lid on for 30 minutes. The mushrooms will make their own juice. Thicken with a small amount of cornflour and water. Serve on hot wholemeal toast.

mustard and dill sauce

1½ tbsps Dijon mustard
¼ cup non fat yoghurt

juice of ½ lemon
2 tbsps fresh chopped dill

Slowly add yoghurt to mustard, mixing all the time until all the yoghurt has been added. Stir in lemon juice and fold through dill.

plum sauce

1kg plums, stoned
2 onions
bouquet garni
1 cup orange juice

1 cup water
2 teaspoons grated ginger
¼ teaspoon cloves
¼ teaspoon peppercorns

Stir fry onions in a small amount of water for 2 minutes. Add plums, orange juice, water, ginger, cloves and peppercorns. Cook over low heat, stirring regularly, for 1 hour or until mixture has reduced and thickened. Pour into sterilised jars and seal. Allow to cool and refrigerate.

ricotta sauce

1 small onion
450g ricotta cheese
1 small tin tomato puree

½ small tin tomato paste
600ml water or apple juice
black pepper to taste

Saute onion, add ricotta cheese, stir in tomato puree, tomato paste and water or apple juice to blend. Mix with a wooden spoon until the ricotta cheese resembles coarse sand. Season with black pepper to taste. Cook slowly over a low flame for 45 minutes.

This sauce is excellent with pasta, over chicken or fish. For a variation, add some chopped fresh parsley or basil.

sweet and sour sauce

1 tin vegetable juice
½ cup unsweetened pineapple juice
½ cup unsweetened pineapple
2 tbsps wine vinegar

black pepper
1 teaspoon cornflour or 2 tbsps tomato paste
½ cup red and green chopped pepper

Combine all ingredients, stirring frequently, and bring to the boil. Boil gently until sauce thickens. Garnish with parsley or chives.

tomato pepper sauce

1 green pepper sliced into rings
½ cup finely sliced celery
½ medium onion finely chopped
1½ cups water

1x425g tin whole tomatoes in natural juice
2 tbsps tomato paste
3 drops tabasco sauce
2 spring onions finely chopped

Lightly cook pepper, celery and onion in water until soft. Add all other ingredients and simmer for 10 minutes. Liquid should reduce to create a sauce thick enough for serving.

tomato relish

1.5kg ripe tomatoes
500g mild onions
2 cups unsweetened orange juice
3 teaspoons curry powder

¼ teaspoon chilli powder
1 tbsp dry mustard
2 cups wine or cider vinegar
1 cup raisins or sultanas (optional)

Skin tomatoes and remove seeds. Cut into cubes. Peel onions, chop finely. Place tomatoes, onions and orange juice into a large saucepan. Combine curry powder, chilli powder and mustard with a small amount of orange juice. Add this to the tomato and onions and add vinegar. Slowly bring to the boil over a low heat. Boil for 5 minutes. Reduce heat and simmer for an hour or until mixture has thickened. Pour relish into sterilised jars, cool and seal. Store in the refrigerator.

tomato sauce

2 cloves garlic crushed
1 onion finely diced
1kg tomatoes peeled, seeded and chopped
2 cups unsweetened orange juice
1 cup grated carrot
pinch mace

½ teaspoon dried oregano
1 tbsp finely chopped fresh
basil or 1 teaspoon dried
1 tbsp finely chopped fresh parsley
2 teaspoons finely grated orange rind
1 cup dry white wine or chicken stock

Place all ingredients in a large saucepan. Slowly bring to the boil. Boil for 5 minutes. Lower heat and simmer until sauce thickens. Pour into sterilised jars, cool and refrigerate.

white sauce

1 cup skim milk
2 tbsps cornflour

black pepper to taste

Pour all but 2 tbsps milk into a saucepan and bring to the boil. Mix cornflour with remaining milk until smooth. Just as bubbles appear prior to boiling, add the paste mixture and beat well. Season with black pepper.

Some Variations:
2 tbsps grated low fat cheese
2 tbsps chives chopped
1 tbsp parsley chopped

2 teaspoons Dijon mustard
2 teaspoons dill weed chopped
2 teaspoons mint chopped
squeeze of lemon

spreads

These spreads are a substitute for the artificially coloured, sugar-loaded jams commercially available.

apple spread

220g dried apples
3 cups unsweetened pineapple juice
½ lemon

2 teaspoons lemon rind
2 teaspoons cinnamon

Combine all ingredients in a large saucepan and simmer over gentle heat until apples are soft. Puree the mixture in a blender and pour into sterilised jars. When cool, seal and store in the refrigerator.

apricot fruit spread

125g dried apricots
90g dried apples

60g raisins
3½ cups unsweetened orange juice

Combine all ingredients in a large saucepan and simmer over gentle heat until fruit is soft. Puree the mixture in a blender and pour into sterilised jars. When cool, seal and store in the refrigerator.

chicken spread

1 cup minced cooked chicken
1 tbsp mild grated onion
1 tbsp finely chopped parsley
1 cup minced blanched almonds

3 tbsps mayonnaise
pinch dried thyme
1 teaspoon lemon juice

Place all ingredients in a food processor and blend well until smooth. Pour into a small pot and refrigerate. Serve with wholemeal toast fingers or fresh wholemeal bread.

date and apple chutney

4 medium cooking apples peeled, cored and grated
500g seeded dates choped
2 onions finely chopped
1 cup raisins, sultanas or apricots
1 teaspoon chilli powder

2 cups unsweetened orange juice
6 whole cloves
¼ teaspoon ground allspice
1½ cups wine or cider vinegar

Place all ingredients in a large saucepan and bring slowly to the boil over a low heat. Simmer, stirring occasionally for 1 hour or until a thick, soft consistency. Spoon into sterilised hot jars and seal when cold. Store in the refrigerator. The flavour will improve if left for at least a week before using.

This is an excellent savoury spread for sandwiches, or use as a dip for vegetable and fruit platters, or as a chutney with chicken and fish vegetable loaves.

plum spread

1kg plums
4 cups orange juice

rind of 1 orange finely grated

Place all ingredients in a saucepan and slowly bring to the boil. Let simmer on gentle heat until liquid has reduced and plums are quite mushy. Remove stones, mash pulp with a potato masher. Pour into sterilised jars and seal when cooled.

pear and orange spread

500g dried pears
1 cup unsweetened orange juice
1 cup water

¼ teaspoon nutmeg
¼ teaspoon mixed spice
rind of 1 orange

Chop pears into small pieces. Place in a saucepan. Add all other ingredients. Slowly bring to the boil and gently simmer until pears are soft and at least half the liquid has been reduced. Remove from heat and mash with a potato masher. Pour into sterilised jars, let cool, seal and keep in the refrigerator.

salmon and cucumber spread

1 small can salmon in water drained
½ cucumber peeled and seeded
½ small capsicum seeded

lemon juice to taste
paprika to taste
finely chopped parsley (optional)

Place all ingredients except parsley in a food processor and blend well until smooth. Pour into a small pot and refrigerate. Parsley can be folded through before pouring into pot if desired.

Serve with wholemeal toast triangles or wholewheat crackers.

savoury spread

250g ripe tomatoes skinned, seeded and chopped
1 tbsp grated onion
1 tbsp grated low fat cheese
1 tbsp non fat yoghurt

1 teaspoon mixed dried herbs
black pepper to taste
⅛ teaspoon cayenne pepper
wholemeal breadcrumbs

Put all ingredients except breadcrumbs in a saucepan. Slowly bring to the boil and boil for 1 minute. Remove from heat. Beat in wholemeal breadcrumbs to make a paste consistency. Store in the refrigerator.

steak paste

500g topside steak
1 bay leaf
1 tbsp water

½ teaspoon black pepper,
ground mace and nutmeg
¼ teaspoon cayenne pepper

Chop steak into small pieces. Remove all fat. Put all ingredients into a heatproof dish with 1 tbsp water. Cover and steam gently for 3 hours. When cool, mince finely in a food processor. Bind with a squeeze of lemon juice. Store in an airtight jar in the refrigerator.

strawberry spread

4 granny smith apples
250g strawberries
2 cups unsweetened orange juice

½–1 teaspoon cinnamon
rind of 1 orange (optional)

Peel and core apples. Slice finely or grate and place in saucepan. Wash and hull strawberries and add to apples. Add orange juice, cinnamon and orange rind. Slowly bring to the boil and gently boil for approx 40 minutes or until liquid and fruit become thick. Pour into sterilised jars. Cool and seal. Once the seal is opened, the strawberry jam should be kept refrigerated.

stuffings

Stuffings will add interest to a meat dish while cutting down the actual quantity of meat you are eating. They will also make a stuffed vegetable a talking piece for the table.

apricot and walnut stuffing

60g dried apricots chopped
3-4 sticks celery finely chopped
125g walnuts finely chopped

1¼ cups wholemeal breadcrumbs
1 tbsp chopped parsley
2 spring onions finely sliced (white part only)

Combine all ingredients. Bind with 1 unbeaten egg white.

parsley stuffing

3 cups wholemeal breadcrumbs
185g shallots
½ cup chopped parsley

black pepper
egg white

Combine all ingredients. When boiling a chicken, use this stuffing to enhance the end flavour.

fennel stuffing

1 small white onion diced
1 cup soft wholemeal breadcrumbs
black pepper

2 tbsps chopped fennel leaves
2 tbsps non fat yoghurt

Combine all ingredients. This stuffing is excellent with fish.

potato and parsley stuffing

1 medium white onion diced
250g mashed potato
125g buckwheat

60g toasted unsalted cashews (optional)
black pepper
8 tbsps chopped parsley

Combine all ingredients.

rice stuffing with herbs

1 cup cooked brown rice
1 medium white onion diced
black pepper

3 tbsp non-fat yoghurt
6 tbsps chopped fresh herbs
(chervil, tarragon, dill, mint, parsley and chives)

Combine all ingredients. Use to stuff peppers, tomatoes, zucchini, squash or cabbage leaves, and chicken.

sage and onion stuffing

1 medium white onion diced
125g soft wholemeal grain breadcrumbs
black pepper

3 tbsps chopped fresh sage or 2 teaspoons dried
1 egg white
4 tbsps skim milk or 3 tbsps non-fat yoghurt

Combine all ingredients.

picnic suggestions

caraway and pumpkin pasties (p. 55)
chicken drumsticks (p. 57)
health sandwiches (p. 104)
sesame scone roll (p. 90)
garden salad (p. 35)
la fiesta salad served in lettuce cups (p. 35)

Sweets
apple rhubarb slice (p. 84)
apple cake (p. 84)
strawberries in orange (p. 81)

dinner party suggestions

1 • tomato sorbet (p. 22)
   • kokanda (spicy African fish dish) (p. 61)
       served with sesame greens (p. 37)
       and mushroom and beanshoots salad (p. 35)
   • apple and date cake (p. 76)

2 • pumpkin soup with basil (p. 29)
     cold chicken and carrot loaf (p. 55)
     served with beetroot mould (p. 33)
     and orange coleslaw (p. 36)
   • steamed fruit pudding (p. 79)
      with ice cream or custard (p. 82) or (p. 112)

3 • salmon dip and platter of vegetables (p. 20)
   • spaghetti (p. 66)
   • strawberry ice cream cake (p. 81)

4 • minestrone (p. 28)
   • potato flan (p. 62)
      served with tomato moulds in lettuce cups (p. 38)
   • fresh fruit and yoghurt (p. 78)

5 • cheesey pear (p. 19)
   • hot curried vegetables (p. 69)
      served with • rice
              • tossed green salad
              • bowl of chilled apple slices
              • bowl of cucumber yoghurt
              • cubes of banana in coconut
   • watermelon sorbet (p. 22)

6 • savoury rock melons (p. 21)
   • whole stuffed cabbage (p. 54)
   • sunshine coast fruit salad (p. 82)

index